MAR 0 7 2001	DATE DUE		
JAN 2 9 2011			
ILL 10/9/12			
ILL 2/29/14			

Jesus gave his disciples (students) power over all manner of diseases; and the Bible was written in order that all peoples, in all ages, should have the same opportunity to become students of the Christ, Truth.

Mary Baker Eddy

EX LIBRIS

COURTESY OF THE FIRST CHURCH OF CHRIST, SCIENTIST

Mary Baker Eddy

THE DISCOVERER

Mary Baker Eddy

BY CYNTHIA PARSONS

VERMONT SCHOOLHOUSE PRESS

THE DISCOVERER: MARY BAKER EDDY

Printed in the United States of America.

First Edition

The photograph of Mary Baker Eddy opposite the title page, as well as three of the photographs in the Scrapbook section of this book are used with the generous permission of The First Church of Christ, Scientist in Boston, Massachusetts and are credited on the photographs. The other photographs in the Scrapbook section are largely from the collection of The Longyear Museum in Chestnut Hill, Massachusetts (and are credited on the photographs) and are also used with their generous permission. The photographs throughout the text of the book as well as several in the Scrapbook are owned by the author.

The illustrations on pages 1, 5, and 9, and the illustration of the steamboat in the Scrapbook, were done by Alice De Caprio. The illustration of the Bow homestead in the Scrapbook was done by Danis Collett Mutchler. The photograph of the author with Norma Heller on page 133 was done by Teresa Heller.

Copies of this book may be ordered directly from:

Enfield Publishing and Distributing Co., Inc.
P.O. Box 699
Enfield, NH 03748
Phone: 603-632-7377

U.S. $20 / Canada $28
ISBN 1-892286-009
Library of Congress Control Number: 00-134630

CONTENTS

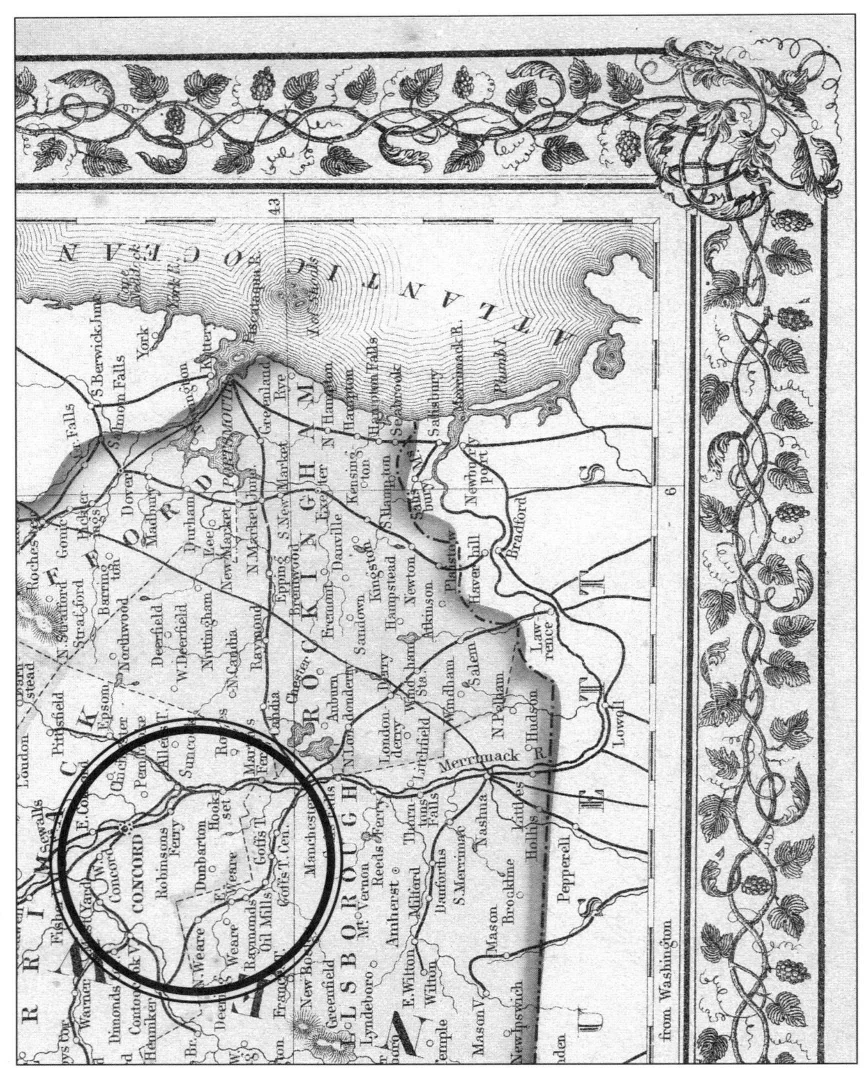

Section of 1874 map showing southern New Hampshire.

Mary Baker Eddy was born and raised in Bow, New Hampshire, just south of Concord. As an adult, she returned to Concord for several years where she accomplished some of her most important work as the Discoverer and Founder of Christian Science.

The Discoverer: Mary Baker Eddy

What a woman!

✣ In 1866, after years of experiments, she discovered the Science behind Jesus' healings, and began healing the same way Jesus did. Then she taught other people how to heal using scientific prayers. No other woman has ever done this.

✣ She wrote a textbook about her discovery more than 125 years ago that people are still buying today. Total sales have reached nearly nine million copies, and it's been translated into seventeen languages. No other woman has ever done this.

✣ Her book, *Science and Health with Key to the Scriptures*, used, in 1906, a larger vocabulary than any other writer except William Shakespeare. No other woman had ever done this.

✣ She founded a church more than 100 years ago that today has congregations in seventy-one nations around the world. No other woman has ever done this.

✣ She founded a college of metaphysics that has taught more than 5,000 Christian Scientists how to heal through prayer and how to teach others to heal through prayer. No other woman has ever done this.

✣ She ordained her book, *Science and Health*, and the Bible, to be the pastors of the Christian Science Church: books, not people. No other woman has ever done this.

✣ She founded a publishing house more than 100 years ago that still circulates a weekly magazine, a monthly magazine, quarterly magazines in twelve languages, an international daily newspaper, and her own seventeen books. No other woman has ever done this.

None of this was easy going for Mary Baker Eddy. Time and again she was so sick that her family thought she would die. Often she couldn't go to school, and she didn't go to college.

She was even too weak physically to take care of her own son when she was a young mother.

Her first husband died before their son was born. Her second husband lied to her and abandoned her when she was sick and penniless. Her third husband died after they had been married only five years.

After she wrote her best-selling textbook, others copied what she had discovered and claimed that they had made their discoveries before she had made hers.

People told her they would help her by selling her book and then kept the sales money for themselves.

Many of her friends became her enemies and, when she was famous, tried to take her money away from her. Newspapers reported her dead when she was still alive, and even her son, along with several others, tried to take over her church and personal wealth by claiming she was mentally unfit.

But she won the major battles.

How? Read on to find out.

Cynthia Parsons
Chester, Vermont

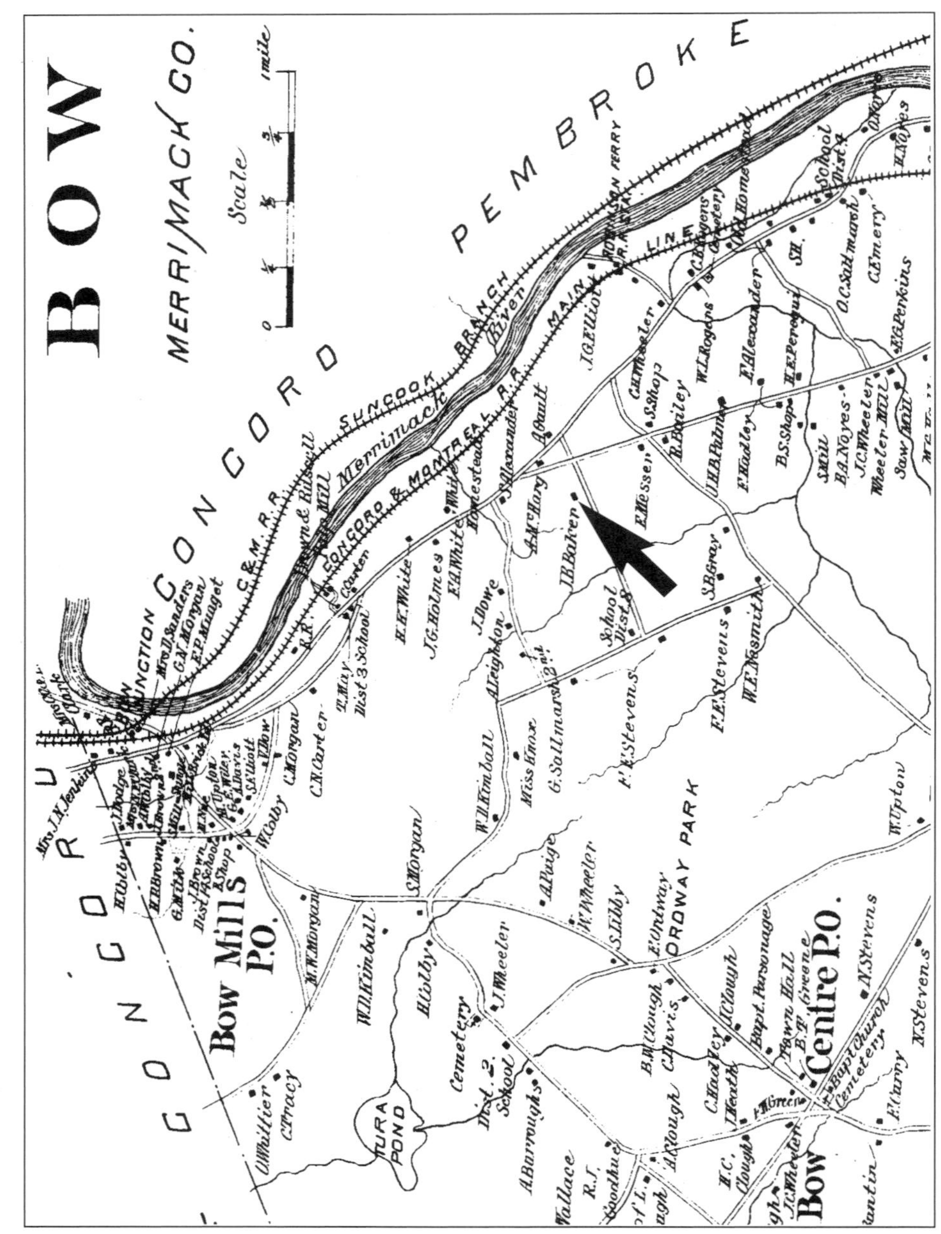

1892 map of
Bow, New Hampshire
with the Baker
homestead.

CHAPTER ONE

Farming and Schooling

"Please remember to get some pine knots this morning, Mary," her grandmother reminded her.

"Mother, please help me on with my coat and boots."

And from her grandmother, "Don't forget your hat, and a scarf to cover your ears."

Then father poked his head in the door and called out, "Tell Mary she needs to get some pine knots before the storm."

"I'm coming father."

And her practical mother, not wanting dirt and snow brought into the house, told her husband, "Put the pine knot basket by the front door so Mary can fill it, and one of the boys can bring it in when it's full and too heavy for Mary."

As she went out into the pine forest, Mary Baker, then six years old, youngest of six children, with two brothers and three sisters, sang hymns to herself. "Joy to the world . . ." she began, then changed the words: "Joy to gather pine knots, and see them in the fire."

Little Mary, born July 16, 1821, was not only the youngest child on the Baker farm but also was somewhat frail and very thin with

delicate features and big striking eyes. All her life (for nearly 90 years!), whenever anyone described her, it was the eyes that made the greatest impression. They changed color: hazel, almost brown, blue, blue grey, bright blue.

The Baker farm was on a New Hampshire hillside a few miles south of Concord on the west side of the Merrimack River. When Mary was six years old, her sister Martha was eight and Abigail was eleven; her brother George was fifteen, Albert seventeen, and Samuel nineteen.

This picture of a typical New England farm scene is from the 1879 edition of *The McGuffey Reader*.

Gathering pine knots was Mary's special job. She didn't do the milking, nor clean up the stalls from the cows, sheep, and chickens (though she did help collect the eggs). She didn't chop or split wood, and in the summers she didn't turn over the garden soil or cut the hay or pitch it up into the barn. She didn't harness the oxen, but she did move freely among them. She did help harvest the apples, peaches, pears, and cherries that grew in the Baker orchard.

Now, a pine knot is a very special bit of wood used to burn overnight in a stove or fireplace. Where the branch comes out from a pine tree high off the ground, the wood twists and doubles up. When the branch is old and dead, the wind will knock it down, and that part of the branch nearest the trunk of the tree generally forms what farmers call a "knot." The pine knot is special. It has a lot of pitch (sap) in it; but it is dense also, and therefore takes longer to burn, and because of the pitch gives off a good amount of heat.

Since it burns more slowly in the fire, if the coals are banked just right, a pine knot will last overnight, not only helping to keep the house warm but making it easier to rekindle the fire in the morning from the leftover warm coals. Finding the pine knots was a very special chore, one Mary could do to help out the family.

Long after Mary Baker Eddy's discovery of healing through scientific prayer, she wrote to a friend recalling an incident that involved a pine knot and a lesson in honesty.

> *When I was a "wee bit" on returning from school I found a pitch pine knot in the woods and carried it home for I liked to see it blaze in the open fireplace. Mother asked me where I got it? I said, "In Mr. Gault's woods." She said, "Did you ask him for it?" I replied "No." She said "Carry it right back again, Mary, it is stealing for you to do that and God forbids you to steal." I asked, "Must I carry it back now I am tired?" She replied, "Would you have God and mother thinking till tomorrow that you have broken His commandment?"*

"A wee bit" means when Mary was a little girl.

Mary's school was a mile from home.

Peel, *Mary Baker Eddy: The Years of Discovery*, P. 10.

Mary Baker was a farmer's daughter through and through. She was also a New Hampshire New Englander, born during the time when the United States of America had but twenty-four states. New Hampshire was one of the original thirteen. Both the Bakers and Ambroses (her mother's family) had lived in the area around Concord, New Hampshire's capital city, for several generations.

When Mary was a toddler, the United States had a population

of 9.6 million; 93 percent lived in rural areas. By the time she was ten years old, 90 percent of the nearly 13 million Americans lived in the country and 10 percent in the cities. The United States was so new that its then president, James Monroe, was only the fifth person to be elected to this office. John Adams, second president, was living at Quincy, Massachusetts, and Thomas Jefferson at Monticello in Virginia. They both died the same day, July 4, 1826. Abraham Lincoln, who was born in 1809, was just twelve years old when Mary was born, and the future Queen Victoria of England was two years old.

While both Sir Walter Scott and Lord Byron were popular authors in 1821, Charles Dickens was only nine years old, and Alfred Lloyd Tennyson only eleven. Edward Everett Hale was born in 1822, and it was his father who pioneered the railroad system in Massachusetts. Edward Hale and Mary Baker did not meet until she had discovered Christian Science and he had been the minister of the South Congregational Church in Boston for some ten years. You might have read Dr. Hale's book, *The Man Without a Country*, which he wrote in 1863.

Even when she was still a toddler, it was Mary to whom her older brothers and sisters brought any of the farm animals who were sick. Let a cow have a struggle with a newborn calf, and Mary was called to come and help the little one adjust to life on the Baker farm. If any of the oxen were disturbed, Mary was the one member of the household who could calm them with soothing words.

"She's got a healing touch," her father willingly exclaimed to neighbors and fellow church friends.

While in the early 1800s, about 90 percent of all the children in the twenty-four United States lived in rural areas, most on farms, today, fewer than five percent of the children in the fifty states live on farms. If you are one of those 95 percent, you may be surprised to learn that all the children in the Baker family were expected to spend several hours a day doing chores. There wasn't much talk about it; no constant reminders from the adults. It was a natural activity. Morning and evenings were feeding and cleaning times: everyone in the family participated in feeding and caring for both the animals and the humans.

Milk, for example, didn't turn into butter on its own; nor was it available in a neighborhood store. One of the children would have been in charge of churning the milk until it turned to butter, of feeding the waste from the churn to the appropriate animals, and cleaning and storing the churn to be ready for the next time butter needed to be made.

After the milk was taken from the cow by hand-squeezing the udders, it would be poured into the top of a tall wooden churn, and after the top had been put on tightly one of the children would turn a handle both back and forth and up and down. After some twenty to thirty minutes, the "butter" globs would begin to separate from a watery milk. Next the butter would be taken out and placed into molds in a cool place to harden. Perhaps in an ice box.

Most probably the Bakers cut blocks of ice from a nearby

pond in mid winter and stored the ice in a shed, covering the ice with sawdust from their sawmill. This ice could last all through a hot New Hampshire summer. The Baker family set up a sawmill at the bottom of their hillside property close to the Merrimack River. In this way, they could use boats to move the processed lumber. Their sawmill was the first one built in New Hampshire.

The Baker farmhouse didn't have a bathroom inside. It didn't have a furnace. It didn't have a telephone or radio or television or electric clock. It had a shed attached to the back of the house with a place for the chickens and some of the baby sheep and other farm animals. It wasn't until the turn of the century, 1900, that rural areas of New England began to get both electricity and telephone service. And it wasn't until 1930 that some 90 percent of all the farms in New England had electric power and some 80 percent had telephones.

The Baker farmhouse had one fireplace, and an iron hook in it on a swing so that a pot of soup or stew or beans could heat up while the fire was warming the room. It had places next to the chimney where bread and other foods could be kept warm. It had a cookstove heated with pieces of wood from the Bakers' own woodlot, with a flat top where the teakettle kept water hot to make tea and cocoa and where soups, stews, and baked beans also could be set to simmer.

Homes were lit with kerosene lamps and heated by stoves and fireplaces. That's why the pine knots were important. Certainly, one of the jobs little Mary could do was to clean the glass chimneys of the kerosene lamps. You see, smoke smudged them, and unless they were cleaned the family wouldn't be able to see well in the evenings to read and do needlework.

While the Baker girls—Abigail, Martha, and Mary—didn't do the heavy farm chores, they, and the hired girl who lived with them, did all the sewing for the family, starting with patterns through to the finished product. They did the mending for the boys and men as well. They knit the hats and mittens.

The sewing machine had not been invented when Mary was a little girl. The very first machine, designed by Elias Howe in Massachusetts, got its first patent in 1846, when Mary was twenty-five years old.

About the same time, a man named Isaac Singer began designing a sewing machine, and with the help of Edward Clark, by 1854, sewing machines were in production, and salesmen were going house to house demonstrating and selling them. The first ones had to be powered by one's own foot by stepping on a piece of metal and pumping it over and over and over in order for the pulley to pull the needle up and down.

Probably the men prepared the vegetable garden using their oxen to pull the plow and disk, but it was the girls who sowed the seeds, pulled the weeds, harvested the vegetables, and prepared them for winter storage. The Bakers planted several kinds of potatoes. Some of the smaller varieties had to be eaten as soon as they were ready, but "keepers," such as baking potatoes, needed to be put carefully into sawdust and placed where it was dry and they would not freeze. Such a place was known as a "root cellar."

Not only potatoes but also carrots, beets, squash, and parsnips needed to be harvested and stored in sawdust for the winter.

Other fruits and vegetables, like rhubarb and tomatoes, had to be cooked and put into jars and stored where it was cool, but not cold enough to freeze. To keep the food from spoiling, they melted some of the tallow, or fat, when they butchered a cow and they poured it on top of the fruit or vegetable. When it hardened, it covered the food and kept out the air.

Of course, anything that wouldn't spoil while frozen was easy for the Baker family to take care of. (Blueberries are nearly as good to eat thawed after being frozen as they are when they are fresh picked; *nearly*). By the end of October, up the hill in Bow, New Hampshire, the temperature at night would go below freezing, and fairly soon both day and night would be colder than 32 degrees Fahrenheit.

What did the Baker children wear when they did their farm chores? When they went to school? When they went to church? What did the adults wear? The boys and the men wore overalls for work, school, and visits to other farms. The men got dressed up to go to church: pants, fancy shirts, jackets, and hats.

Of course, the youngest Baker boy and girl got the most hand-me-downs, but generally farm boys and men had but one "good" suit for church and special occasions.

The girls and women always wore dresses. Always. They wore simple dresses made of sturdy material when they did farm chores and when the girls went to school. But for church, just like the boys and men, they had special clothes, fancy dresses made of pretty materials, and they wore fancy hats. It would be more than one hundred years before women began wearing pants anywhere but on their farms or inside their houses!

These girls are dressed in fancy clothes typical of the style worn when Mary was a young girl.

Boys and girls wore sturdy shoes and farm boots. These boots, often made of hard rubber, were never allowed in the house when they were dirty, but each wearer was expected to scrape off all dirt and clean them with water and then place them where they could get dry and warm before the next outing.

Almost all the clothes the boys, men, girls, and women wore were made by the women. Even when Mary was much older and rich and famous, and had a seamstress to take care of her clothes, she sometimes still did a bit of fixing with needle and thread.

In all, there were ten people living in the Baker home when Mary was born. Six children, her parents, her grandmother, and a girl who helped with the heavier household chores. In Mary's book, *Retrospection and Introspection*, (P. 4) written when she was seventy years old, is this description of the Baker homestead.

> *[My] venerable grandmother had thirteen children, the youngest of whom was my father, Mark Baker, who inherited the homestead, and with his brother, James Baker, he inherited my grandfather's farm of about five hundred acres, lying in the adjoining towns of Concord and Bow, in the State of New Hampshire.*

One hundred acres of the old farm are still cultivated and owned [1891] by Uncle James Baker's grandson, brother of the Hon. Henry Moore Baker of Washington, D.C.

The farm-house, situated on the summit of a hill, commanded a broad picturesque view of the Merrimack River and the undulating lands of three townships. But change has been busy. Where once stretched broad fields of bending grain waving gracefully in the sunlight, and orchards of apples, peaches, pears, and cherries shone richly in the mellow hues of autumn, — now the lone night-bird cries, the crow caws cautiously, and wandering winds sigh low requiems through dark pine groves. Where green pastures bright with berries, singing brooklets, beautiful wild flowers, and flecked with large flocks and herds, covered areas of rich acres, — now the scrub-oak, poplar, and fern flourish.

By the time Mary was five years old, her brother Albert was sixteen and getting ready to go to Dartmouth College in Hanover, New Hampshire. He taught school to make money for necessary books and school supplies, and his most avid pupil was his youngest sister, Mary. Often Mary was too ill to go out and either walk the mile to school or even ride on the wagon pulled by the oxen, so Albert tutored her, discovering that she was eager to keep up with his classical reading (Shakespeare's plays, for example) and his study of Latin. She also studied a smattering of Greek and Hebrew along with him.

Her grandmother, a great storyteller, lived with them, and it was

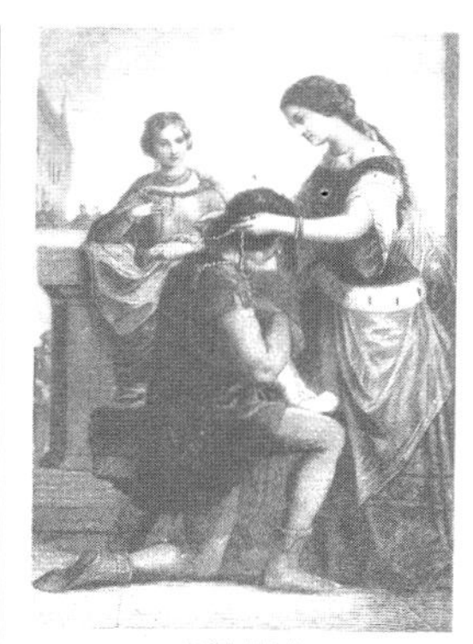

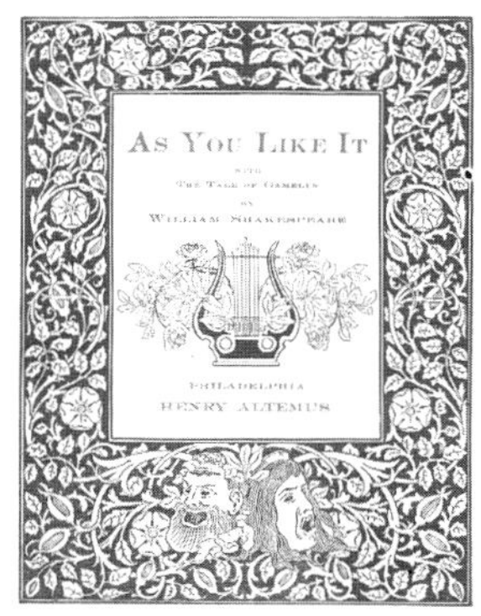

Many years later, Mrs. Eddy would quote from this play of Shakespeare's in her book *Science and Health*:

Sweet are the uses of adversity; / Which, like the toad, ugly and venomous, / Wears yet a precious jewel in his head.

Shakespeare
As You Like It

she who encouraged Mary to memorize hundreds and hundreds of lines of verse from classic literature. Her mother and her brother Albert also encouraged her to write poetry, and even helped her submit them for publication in local newspapers and weekly journals.

This is one she wrote and had published locally. Later, it was included in a book of some fifty poems that appeared in 1910 in *Poetical Works*, by Mary Baker Eddy, published by the church she founded.

The last stanza provides the point of the poem and gives a glimmer of her spiritual outlook; the more remarkable since it is a poem by a child not yet in her teens, and was published in a local newspaper not as the work of a "child," but of a poet.

Autumn

Quickly earth's jewels disappear;
The turf, whereon I tread,
Ere Autumn blanch another year,
May rest above my head.

Touched by the finger of decay
Is every earthly love;
For joy, to shun my weary way,
Is registered above.

The languid brooklets yield their sighs,
  A requiem o'er the tomb
Of sunny days and cloudless skies,
  Enhancing autumn's gloom.

The wild winds mutter, howl, and moan,
  To scare my woodland walk,
And frightened fancy flees, to roam
  Where ghosts and goblins stalk.

The cricket's sharp, discordant scream
  Fills mortal sense with dread;
More sorrowful it scarce could seem;
  It voices beauty fled.

Yet here, upon this faded sod, —
  O happy hours and fleet, —
When songsters' matin hymns to God
  Are poured in strains so sweet,

My heart unbidden joins rehearse,
  I hope it's better made,
When mingling with the universe,
  Beneath the maple's shade.

Miscellaneous Writings, Pg. 395-396.

It's probably true to say that Mary was spoiled by all her family; sisters as well as brothers and cousins, along with the adults. She wasn't physically strong, so she deserved concerned attention from those who were. But she had two positive traits that endeared her to everyone—young and old—who knew her as a child.

She was a peacemaker. She was the one to help settle disputes among the children. She was the one whom brothers and sisters turned to for solace and comfort when they were hurt. This story about her must be true; many who were there that day have told it. Suddenly in the school yard during a recess a strange-looking man appeared, someone who had escaped from a nearby facility for those who were mentally deranged. He appeared confused and frightened; the schoolchildren were even more frightened and began screaming and running in circles, adding to the man's distress.

Not Mary. She went right over to him, took his hand, found out his name, told him hers, and led him peacefully over to the teacher.

The other trait was her love of learning. She devoured the books her older brothers and sisters brought from school. When anyone came to the farm, she loved to learn from them about their special interests. While the other children might go outside or to the barn to play, Mary would curl up in a corner listening and learning from the discussions held by the adults.

Many who came to visit the Baker farm up the hill from the Merrimack River were scholars, particularly friends of her brilliant brother Albert. Many were church or town officials, and ever

so many were relatives. Mary's father had nine older brothers and sisters; her mother had six siblings. There were scores of cousins who lived nearby, and while a great deal of the talk must have been about farming, politics and public affairs were also part of an evening's discussions.

Mary's early growing years were exciting years for New Hampshire, New England, the United States, and the world. The Industrial Revolution was in full swing, substituting mechanization for hand tools, starting in England, moving to Continental Europe, and then across the Atlantic to the former colonies. The United States was home to exciting free thinkers, willing to challenge long-held political, social, and economic traditions. Many of these visionaries were New Englanders.

Mary Baker, the religious revolutionary, couldn't have come at a better time, or to a more appropriate environment. The soil, to use a farm analogy, had been prepared, and when she made her discovery in the middle of the 19th century, people in New England first, and then gradually around the world, gave her writings serious consideration.

While women had to wait many more years to get the right to vote in national elections, by 1847 New England was leading the way, giving women some property rights: Massachusetts and Maine (1844), Connecticut (1845), New Hampshire (1846), and Vermont (1847). Some southern states still had not given women any property rights one hundred years later.

Slavery was outlawed first in Vermont (1777), then a few years later in Connecticut, Rhode Island, Massachusetts, and Maine. New Hampshire specifically banned slavery and declared Negroes full citizens of the state on July 26, 1857. But long before, in 1789, New Hampshire's Negroes could no longer be taxed as property. Yet the first United States census, taken in 1792, listed 150 slaves in New Hampshire.

My soul an't yours, Mas'r!
You haven't bought it,
— ye can't buy it.

Harriet Beecher Stowe
UNCLE TOM'S CABIN

The new United States, forming the most radical democratic government anywhere in the world, was an exciting place to be in the mid 1800s.

New England was home to many reformers. Henry David Thoreau (1817-1862), essayist and poet, was revolutionizing the way the natural environment should be perceived and preserved. Amos Bronson Alcott (1799-1888), educator and philosopher, and his daughter Louisa May (1832-1888), author and reformer, were challenging philosophical and social conventions, shaking them to their very core.

A hymn written by Harriet Beecher Stowe would one day be included in the *Christian Science Hymnal*. It is still sung today. The hymn begins, "Still, still with Thee when purple morning breaketh . . ."

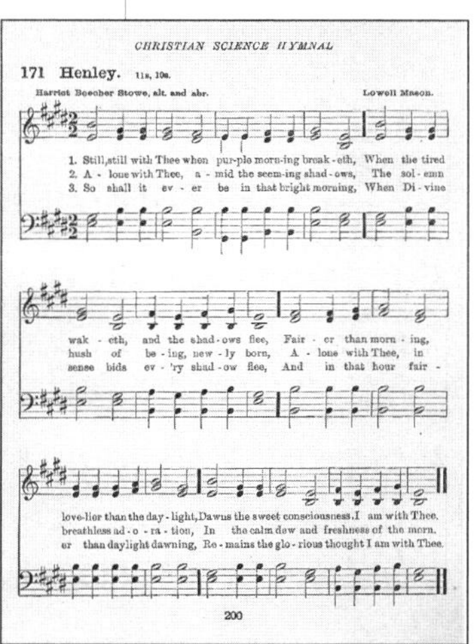

Another New England contemporary of Mary Baker, Harriet Beecher Stowe (1811-1896), through her writings encouraged the entire nation to think deeply about the emancipation of all Negroes and mixed-blood descendants.

Electricity and water were harnessed during this period as never before. Arduous farm chores, always done by hand, were now accomplished with the help of machinery. New ways of doing things came from a willingness to think new thoughts. And Mary Baker—apparently from her earliest years—was a radical thinker, willing to examine many points of view.

Mary read and studied her brother Albert's college texts, kept a diary, and wrote stories and poetry every chance she got. The Bible was an important book in the Baker home. You may be surprised to learn that Mary's father would not ever let any of the daughters or his wife or even his own mother read aloud from the Bible in the evenings.

The women and girls could read the Bible to themselves and talk about what they were learning from the Bible among themselves, but public reading of the Bible was reserved for the men. The Baker boys were not Bible readers, so it was mostly her father who read the Bible aloud, giving his thoughts as the "correct" interpretation. One biblical injunction subscribed to by Mark Baker caused an enormous blowup between Mary and her father and spread out to the male elders of the church. But that story comes in Chapter Two.

When Mary was twelve, she wrote what we might call a "ditty" she titled, "Resolutions for the Morning." It's eight stanzas long, but I'll here quote just two.

I'll form resolutions with strength from on high,
   Such physical laws to obey,
As reason with appetite, pleasures deny,
   That *health*, may my efforts repay.

I'll go to the altar of God and pray,
   That the reconciled smiles of His son

Peel, *Mary Baker Eddy: The Years of Discovery*, P. 25.

May illumine my path through the wearisome day,
  And *cheer* me with *hope* when 'tis done.

It is wondrous to think about this little farm-girl pondering the meaning of such concepts as "health," "God," "prayer," and "hope," knowing what she finally accomplished some thirty-four years later when she discovered how prayer actually does heal both physical and mental illnesses.

Mary read and studied and committed to memory pages and pages of three books written by Lindley Murray: the *Introduction to the English Reader*, *The English Reader*, and the *Sequel to the English Reader*. They were filled with 18th Century prose and poetry by such famous authors as Addison, Goldsmith, Johnson, Milton, and Pope. The vocabulary was not easy for an adult, much less for a child. But Mary, first with brother Albert's help, and later with local scholars, showed enormous aptitude for understanding complex ideas.

The same author also wrote grammar books that Mary studied. On the title page of the 1809 edition of *Murray's Grammar* is a quotation from Dr. Hugh Blair, whose writings appear in the *Reader*. It is clear from Mary's later writings after her discovery that she agreed with Dr. Blair that: "They who are learning to compose and arrange their sentences with accuracy and order, are learning, at the same time, to think with accuracy and order."

AN
ENGLISH GRAMMAR:
COMPREHENDING
THE PRINCIPLES AND RULES
OF THE
LANGUAGE,
ILLUSTRATED BY
APPROPRIATE EXERCISES,
AND
A KEY TO THE EXERCISES.

BY LINDLEY MURRAY.

"They who are learning to compose and arrange their sentences with accuracy and "order, are learning, at the same time, to think with accuracy and order." .... BLAIR.

IN TWO VOLUMES.

VOLUME II.

THE SECOND EDITION, IMPROVED.

York:
Printed by Thomas Wilson & Son, High-Ousegate,
FOR LONGMAN, HURST, REES, AND ORME; AND DARTON AND HARVEY, LONDON:
FOR WILSON AND SON, AND R. AND W. SPENCE, YORK: AND
FOR CONSTABLE AND CO. EDINBURGH.
1809.

Title page from an 1809 edition of Lindley Murray's *English Grammar*.

The 1809 edition of Lindley Murray's *English Grammar*.

The following are the titles of some of the essays Mary read in *The English Reader*:

> THE IMPORTANCE OF A GOOD EDUCATION
> ON GRATITUDE
> PIETY AND GRATITUDE ENLIVEN PROSPERITY
> ON FORGIVENESS
> CHARITY
> THE MAN OF INTEGRITY

The Baker Library at Dartmouth College has a copy of the *Sequel to the English Reader* (1811), and it was with some delight I found leaves and flowers still pressed between the pages in this small (7 inches long by 4 inches wide), 366-page hardcover book. The print, as was the custom of the day, is small, and there are some 300 words to a page. The author states on the cover page that the prose and poetry selections are: "Designed to improve the highest class of learners in reading; to establish a taste for just and accurate composition; and to promote the interests of piety and virtue."

Both the prose and the poetry sections are divided into eight parts: narrative, didactic, argumentative, descriptive, pathetic [sad], dialogues, public speeches, and promiscuous [mixed selections]. The appendix contains short biographies of the major writers. Only one is an English woman: Elizabeth Carter (1718-1806), whom the author describes as having, "goodness of heart, mildness of temper, and suavity of manners." She was a scholar of both Latin and Greek. Her "Ode to Wisdom" is in the poetry half of the *Reader*, and in the prose section is an essay by her titled, "Religion and Superstition Contrasted."

We can assume that the young Mary read and thought much about the differences between religion and superstition, since the adult Mary wrote about them.

Joseph Addison (1672-1719), also English, was best known for his prose works, such as the essay in the narrative section of the *Reader* titled: "Endeavours of Mankind To Get Rid of Their Burdens; a Dream," of which Dr. Samuel Johnson said, "This essay of Addison's on the burden of mankind [is] the most exquisite [I] have ever read."

Dr. Hugh Blair (1718-1800), a Scot, a scholar, and a minister, published a collection of his sermons that were extremely popular and were translated into several European languages. A few of these sermons are included in the *Reader*. One that made a particular impression on Mary is titled: "The Folly and Misery of Idleness." In a speech to the members of the Christian Science church in 1900, she declared that "idleness is egotism and animality."

Dr. Samuel Johnson's (1709-1784) prose and poetry fill the pages of this *Reader*. They come from such famous works as "The Rambler" and "The Vanity of Human Wishes." His essays, Murray states, "form a body of ethics; the observations on life and manners, are acute and instructive; and . . . serve to promote the cause of literature."

The following are some of the arithmetic questions Mary and the other younger children had to answer when she went to the school down the hill in Bow, about a mile from the Baker farmhouse. They are in Book I of *The Essentials of Arithmetic*:

- A man makes 4 pairs of shoes in a week. What part of the work does he do in a day?
- If you sleep 1/3 of your time, how many hours do you sleep every week?
- What is 1/365 of 6,429 days?
- Which of these numbers is invisible and exists only in the mind, or is *abstract*?
  5 books 15 $9
- Mary wrote 24 words and misspelled 1/6 of them. How many did she get right?
- Name all the numbers between 3,748 and 3,800 that end in 9.

Mary also memorized much of the text of *Murray's Grammar*. Throughout the book, the author gives examples of grammar that need correcting. For example, he asks the pupil to supply a missing word from a sentence; a word needed to make the sentence grammatically correct. For example:

- *Let us consider the works of nature and art, with proper attention.*

Missing is the word "of." The correct sentence is: "Let us consider the works of nature and of art, with proper attention."

The grammar book is filled with pious statements; that is, sentences and phrases about being good and well-behaved. The following sentence needs correcting:

✣ *She who studies her Glass neglects her Heart*

Missing, of course, is the period at the end of the sentence, but also a comma is missing. Two of the words should be written in lower-case letters. The correct sentence reads:

"She who studies her glass, neglects her heart." The reference to "glass" is, of course, a reference to a mirror.

Now, can you spot the mistakes in the following sentence taken from *Murray's Grammar*?

✣ *Let me repeat it He only is great who has the Habits of Greatness*

According to Mary's grammar book the correct sentence looks like this: "Let me repeat it; — he only is great who has the habits of greatness."

What is wrong in this next sentence?

✣ *The sincere is always esteemed.*

As the grammar book explains, "A verb must agree with its nominative case, in number and person." Thus the correct sentence is: "The sincere are always esteemed."

Very few English grammar teachers today teach students how to parse a sentence, but it was very common when Mary was in school. Children were expected to tell what parts of speech were used, how they were used, and why the words used were chosen.

For the verb, the student should ask himself or herself: "What kind? Mood? Tense? Number? Person? Why? If a participle, why? Active or passive?"

In the following sentences, the word "much" needs parsing. Can you tell from how it is used what part of speech it is?

- Much money is corrupting.
- Think much, and speak little.
- He has seen much of the world, and been much caressed.

Now, you have done the same schoolwork as Mary Baker!

SECOND YEAR'S WORK. 141

187. Hard Words of Greek Origin.

Graph'o = to write; graph'y = writing.

bios	=	life	bi og' ra phy
autos	=	self	au' to graph
cheir	=	hand	chi rog' ra phy
kalos	=	fine	ca lig ra phy
gē	=	earth	ge og ra phy
lithos	=	stone	li thog ra phy
orthos	=	correct	or thog ra phy
photos	=	light	pho tog ra phy
phonos	=	sound	pho nog ra phy
typos	=	type	ty pog ra phy
topos	=	place	to pog ra phy
tele	=	far off	tel' e graph
stenos	=	short	ste nog' ra phy
stereos	=	fixed	ste' re o type

188. Greek Derivatives.

Pol'is = city; pol'us = many; go'nia = angle; cos'mos = world; met'ron = measure; path'os = feeling.

po lite'	me trop' o lis	pol' y gon	ap' a thy
pol' i tics	met ro pol' i tan	oc ta gon	sym pa thy
pol i ti' cian	cos mo pol i tan	hep ta gon	pa thol' o gy
po lice'	cos mop' o lite	di ag' o nal	al lo path' ic
pol' i cy	pol y syl' la ble	trig o nom' e try	ho mœ op a thy
pol ish	pol y no mi al	pol y tech nic	hy dro path ic

189. Greek Derivatives.

Ar'che = rule; graph'o = to write.

mon' arch y	en grave'	pho tog' ra pher
an ar chy	gram' mar	li thog ra pher
ol i garch y	graph ic	tel e graph' ic
ar chi tect	tel e gram	eth nog' ra phy
pa tri arch	di a gram	his to ri og' ra pher
arch bish' op	mon o gram	ty pog' ra pher
arch an gel	par a graph	ty po graph' i cal

Mary did learn a smattering of Greek. This exercise page in Greek derivatives is found in the *English Spelling Book*.

During her brother Albert's time at Dartmouth College, he was given the greatest of undergraduate academic honors: in his junior year he was made a Phi Beta Kappa scholar. And at his graduation, he gave one of the key talks.

Albert spoke at a Literary Festival at Dartmouth about serious matters touching on the laws of life, taking a stand about truth as stronger than evil. Even though Mary was only fourteen, she had thought through with him issues about the impact of "unforgiving" Puritan religious beliefs. Here are four sentences from Albert's graduation talk, but note how very long the third sentence is—eighty-three words! That was typical prose at that time.

> *We see man crawling into existence, weak and helpless at first, the prey of a thousand calamities inseparable from his condition. Increased in strength by uniting into clans and hordes, driven by a resistless fury, we see him pursuing the endless round of mutual destruction. But when we reflect that there is nothing like chance in existence, that the whole universe is governed by a Primitive Intelligence, that the events of human life have their laws, as well as the phenomena of matter, and that it is the nature of error, like that of confusion, to destroy itself in the end, we feel the same assurance in the one case, that truth will prevail over error, as in the other, that order has, and will prevail, over confusion. This is the tendency of things, and no power on earth can resist it.*

Not everyone believed that "there is nothing like chance in existence." Even today, many believe that it is not our own thinking that prevails in our lives, but some kind of chance or luck or pre-existing tendency coming from one's parents and ancestors.

Since what interested Albert in his academic studies was what he shared with the sister eleven years his junior, Mary, too, wrestled with many of the deepest philosophical issues that had concerned learned men and women for ages. And we know from her own later writings that she was positive that there is a "Primitive Intelligence" governing the whole world. That's not what she called it, but again, we're getting ahead of the story.

One by one, Mary's brothers left the farm. Her eldest brother, Samuel, went to the big city of Boston and became a building contractor. He married a young woman from Concord whose older brother, George Washington Glover, feel deeply in love with Mary, as you will learn in Chapter Three.

But Mark Baker, after his mother died and without sons to help him with his large farm, and who lost the help of an older brother who used to have an adjoining farm, decided to move to a smaller farm near the town of Sanbornton, a few miles north of Concord. The family now consisted of Mark and Abigail Baker and their three daughters.

It was typical in farming communities for the girls to go to school in the summer and the boys in the winter. This was due to the fact that farm chores in the winter were slight, but summer seeding and harvesting were dawn-to-dusk work, work, work. Happily for teenager Mary, when the Bakers moved to Sanbornton Bridge, it was in their home that the local schoolteacher boarded, giving Mary an opportunity for tutoring in the long winter evenings. Also, she was well enough the first summer to attend school herself. In addition, her eldest sister, Abigail, was teaching school nearby, so the home was filled with books and ideas—the meat of Mary's joy.

To end this first chapter, here are two verses from a poem Mary wrote when she was about ten years old. Notice how she's really looking forward to accomplishing something special when she's grown up. The title of the poem is "Upward."

> I've watched in the azure the eagle's proud wing,
> His soaring majestic, and feather-some fling —
> Careening in liberty higher and higher —
> Like genius unfolding a quenchless desire.
>
> My course, like the eagle's, oh, still be it high,
> Celestial the breezes that waft o'er the sky!
> God's eye is upon me — I am not alone
> When onward and upward and heavenward borne.

Poems, P. 18.

CHAPTER TWO

Teenage Troubles and Triumphs

✣

Father, I am sorry, but I don't agree with you."

That was it. Mary, who was the most obedient of all Mark Baker's six children, and the one with the most gentle manner, took a stand against him, a stand he found so radical that a battle line was drawn between them.

God's wrath, not God's love, was what appeared to be most important to Mary's father. To "fear" God, as the Bible declares, was not, for Mark Baker, to love Him, but to actually fear Him. To learn about God's love for her, and for all mankind, Mary turned to her mother. Mary was willing to obey God, in fact eager to do so, but what she did not agree with was her father's belief that her brothers and sisters were damned to hell, if not purgatory, by not declaring God as their Savior and joining the church.

For a time, when Mary was thirteen, both her father and the church pastor in Bow refused to allow her to join the church members in profession of her faith unless she agreed with what is called predestination; that is, that God had already decided who would or would not go to hell forever. But she persisted and was allowed to worship along with her parents.

✣

When she was sixteen, she struggled all over again with her father and the church pastor in Sanbornton about this unforgiving nature of God.

Mark Baker believed wholeheartedly, as did the pastor, Reverend Corser, that all people were born in evil, all were evil thinkers, all were damned to hell, until—and unless—they joined the church and got on their physical and mental knees to beg God for forgiveness.

Mary argued that God's love was greater than that, and that it was how one lives and worships God that determines one's destination. She won. She was admitted to full membership as an adult. This was no little victory in her mind. Fifty years later she wrote about what had happened:

> *I was unwilling to be saved, if my brothers and sisters were to be numbered among those who were doomed to perpetual banishment from God. So perturbed was I by the thoughts aroused by this erroneous doctrine, that the family doctor was summoned, and pronounced me stricken with fever. . . .*
>
> *My mother, as she bathed my burning temples, bade me lean on God's love, which would give me rest, if I went to Him in prayer, as I was wont to do, seeking His guidance. I prayed; . . . The fever was gone. . .*
>
> *When the meeting was held for the examination of candidates for membership, I was of course present. . . .*
>
> *I stoutly maintained that I was willing to trust God, and take my chance of spiritual safety with my brothers and*

Retrospection and Introspection, P. 13.

sisters, — not one of whom had then made any profession of religion, — even if my creedal doubts left me outside the doors. . . I could only answer him [the pastor] in the words of the Psalmist: "Search me, O God, and know my heart: try me, and know my thoughts: and see if there be any wicked way in me, and lead me in the way everlasting."

Psalm 139: 23, 24.

This was so earnestly said, that even the oldest church-members wept. After the meeting was over they came and kissed me. To the astonishment of many, the good clergyman's heart also melted, and he received me into their communion, and my protest along with me.

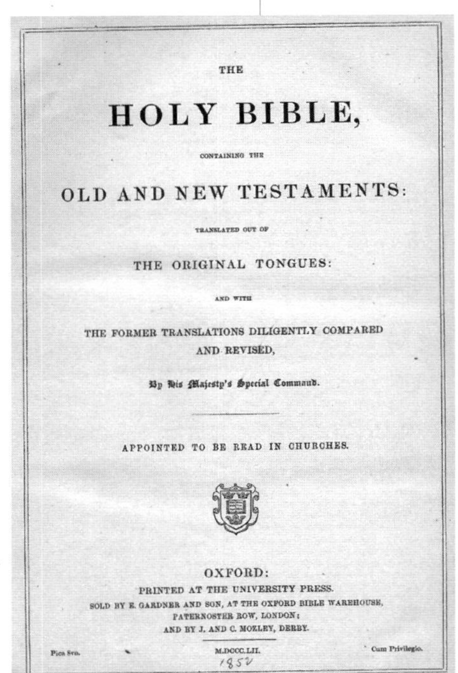
THE
HOLY BIBLE,
CONTAINING THE
OLD AND NEW TESTAMENTS:
TRANSLATED OUT OF
THE ORIGINAL TONGUES:
AND WITH
THE FORMER TRANSLATIONS DILIGENTLY COMPARED
AND REVISED,
By His Majesty's Special Command.

APPOINTED TO BE READ IN CHURCHES.

OXFORD:
PRINTED AT THE UNIVERSITY PRESS.
SOLD BY E. GARDNER AND SON, AT THE OXFORD BIBLE WAREHOUSE,
PATERNOSTER ROW, LONDON;
AND BY J. AND C. MOZLEY, DERBY.

Pica 8vo. M.DCCC.LII. Cum Privilegio.
1852

This is the title page of an 1852 Bible.

That Mary defied her father first when she was thirteen and again at sixteen is absolutely remarkable. Girls, especially, in the 1830s did what their parents told them to do, and believed what their parents told them to believe. If they didn't agree, they kept such radical thoughts to themselves. All who knew Mark Baker spoke of his firmness and of his inflexible positions concerning his religious beliefs.

Now, Mary's father did not state that he had changed his beliefs, but he was content enough to believe in his own daughter's convictions to allow her to have and to hold a view radically different from his own. He could have refused to be a fellow member of any church that would allow her to hold her own views different from those of his and the pastor's. He didn't; instead he honored her original thinking.

Years later Mary wrote about her parents, saying of her father that "He possessed a strong intellect and an iron will." Of her mother, she loved what the Reverend who spoke at her funeral said, "She possessed a strong intellect, a sympathizing heart, and a placid spirit. . . . As a mother, she was untiring in her efforts to secure the happiness of her family." Mrs. Baker also was sure that Mary was very special. Clearly she was different from her sisters and girl cousins in her thirst for knowledge, and it was Mary's mother who urged her to believe the Bible promises when she was the most disturbed.

This is a typical picture that appeared in Bibles when Mary was growing up. The picture is illustrating the early life of Moses. The story is in chapter two, in Exodus, the second book of the Bible.

Mary would one day write, "The First Commandment is my favorite text." (*Science and Health*, P. 340.) It had first been written down by Moses thousands of years before!

It must have been a very difficult time for Mary's mother— trying to maintain a balance between her rigid husband and her determined daughter. She must have been thrilled when her husband and the church officials agreed to disagree with Mary.

The pastor, Reverend Corser, also forgave Mary for holding a religious opinion different from what he believed. He was not only Mary's pastor, but her tutor; he himself was a sound scholar, a graduate of Middlebury College. Of her scholarship he stated publicly: "Bright, good, and pure, aye brilliant! I never before had a pupil with such depth of independence of thought. She has some great future, mark that. She is an intellectual and spiritual genius."

Another triumph coming in her teenage years was the success

of her brother Albert as a scholar. When she was thirteen, he graduated from Dartmouth, and she wrote in her own autobiography about him that, "[He] was reputed one of the most talented, close, and thorough scholars ever connected with that institution."

PHI BETA KAPPA SOCIETY. 41

1834.

*Albert Baker, Esq.,	*Hillsborough.*
Hon. Daniel Clark, LL. D., Sen. U. S. Cong., Judge U. S. Dist. Court.	*Manchester.*
Moses T. Clough, Esq.,	*Ticonderoga, N. Y.*
Rev. William S. Coggin,	*Boxford, Ms.*
Hon. Moody Currier, Councillor, Pres. N. H. Senate.	*Manchester.*
Richard B. Kimball, Esq.,	*New York City.*

Albert Baker's name in the Phi Beta Kappa Society roster.

Albert did not live far from Bow or Sanbornton Bridge while he spent three years studying law in the office of Franklin Pierce, the New Hampshire man who went on to be elected President of the United States. He continued to share books and writings with younger sister Mary, even while he passed the bar exams in both New Hampshire and Massachusetts.

Albert nearly died of some serious illness just after becoming a lawyer, and he came home to be with the family. Mary not only nursed him but once again studied with him, read with him, and had his acute criticism of her own efforts at poetry. He recovered and began a thriving law practice.

When Mary was eighteen, Albert was elected to a two-year term in the New Hampshire Legislature. She was enormously proud that it was he who sponsored—and saw to it that it passed—a bill stopping the imprisoning of persons who were in debt. Before his bill, people who owed money were put in prison where they could earn no money, and yet could not get out until they had paid their debt. This was the kind of terrible injustice Mary despised. How thrilling for her that her brother could do something to stop this absurd situation.

The seal of the State of New Hampshire.

Mary's own health was as fragile as her brother's. She had begun a special diet; the Graham Cure. When she was in her late teenage years, she ate only bread and vegetables and drank only water. When this didn't stop her stomach troubles, she went on the most severe Graham's Cure. She ate just one slice of thin, whole-wheat bread every twenty-four hours, and three hours after the bread she drank one glass of water.

Science and Health, P. 221.

She kept to this radical diet for years and years.

The winter of 1837, both Mary and her sister Martha were ill in bed. After Martha recovered, she wrote Albert about Mary: "In addition to her former diseases, her stomach became most shockingly cankered, and an ulcer collected on her lungs, causing the most severe distress you can conceive of; the physician with the family thought her cure impossible, but she has a good deal recovered for two weeks past, and this morning was carried out to ride."

Peel, *Mary Baker Eddy: The Years of Discovery*, P. 44.

Mary, mind you, was not carried out to ride astride on a horse, but to ride in the Bakers' horse-drawn carriage. In October, Martha wrote again to Albert to report that "Mary's health is gradually advancing on bread and water."

Besides her painful stomach and disturbed lungs, Mary was ill with a problem that the family physician said was due to some sort of nervous disorder. Time and again, family members in attendance were sure she would not recover, but her mother felt the power of prayer, turning always to the Bible to comfort herself and to pray for Mary.

But tragedy struck the Baker home on October 17, 1841. Albert

died. His rival for a seat in the U.S. House of Representatives, Isaac Hill, said: "It is a public calamity." For Mary it was a personal one.

While she loved her other brothers and sisters, none of them shared Albert's interest in spiritual exploration. He was a deep thinker, and, like Mary, wrote analytically and thoughtfully about what he was studying. Like Mary, he was willing to challenge even the most publicly-held ideas in philosophy, religious study, and the law. She was devastated at the loss, yet somehow found a way to keep going.

After Albert's passing, Mary went, even though she was twenty years old, to Sanbornton Academy continuing to read and study classical literature, natural philosophy, logic, and moral science. During a lesson in philosophy, the teacher asked: "What would be left of an orange if you were to throw away the peel, squeeze out the juice, and destroy the seeds and pulp?" One by one the pupils either said they did not know or that nothing would be left. Not Mary. She replied, "There would be left the *thought* of the orange."

Shortly after her brother Albert's passing, a letter about him appeared in a New Hampshire newspaper. It praised his work in the state legislature and also stated: "He had a strong and disciplined intellect. In manner he was always forcible, often eloquent, and at times his lips seemed touched with a coal from the very altar of truth." That spark or "coal" appeared in Mary as well. True, it was nearly extinguished over and over again, but she did go on living and thinking and learning, which led twenty-five years later to her discovery of the Science of Christian healing.

Mary's teenage years were not just filled with sickness. She was able to go to school from time to time, read widely, spend high-quality time with her learned brother, and, with her older sisters, enjoyed an active social life. There were cousins galore getting married, having parties, and visiting each other.

All three Baker girls were popular with other girls and with boys. The oldest, Abigail, was being courted by a member of a prominent Sanbornton Bridge family by the name of Tilton, and after their marriage, the name of the town was changed in 1869 to Tilton. Today, an interstate highway, #93, passes Tilton, New Hampshire, on its way north from Concord to St. Johnsbury, Vermont.

The Baker girls were fashionable; they all sewed with considerable skill, and dressed with care. Better to have one very pretty and fashionable dress than several mediocre frocks. Mary was considered to be not only the most intelligent and the most witty of the three sisters but also the prettiest. Those eyes! How they must have sparkled when she was well enough to be out of bed and enjoying talking, singing, dancing, and playing parlor games.

Girls and women living in New England in the 1800s never wore pants, but always wore dresses and skirts. They might wear what were called "pantaloons." These pants covered girls' and women's legs to the ankle, and sometimes had a strap which went under their foot inside their shoes. But these pants were covered by a skirt, as well as one or two petticoats. What they called a

"petticoat," we call a "slip" today. They wore several layers of clothing in the winter. Both boys and girls wore tightly woven undershirts, and the men wore underpants that went right down to their ankles.

While the Baker family wasn't rich, they also were not poor, and so the three girls—Abigail, Martha, and Mary—could have at least two dresses. One for working on the farm and around the house, most probably always covered by a full-length apron. And one fancier dress to be worn with a hat for church and parties and going visiting.

Keeping their clothes clean was a mighty struggle. No washing machines, no faucets with hot water. Water had to be pumped through a pipe from a spring into the well and then carried in buckets into the Baker house. Then the water had to be heated on the cook stove, and all clothes had to be washed by hand. The Baker girls made their own underclothes as well as their aprons and dresses. And during their monthly periods, they used soft cotton cloths to protect their dresses and washed them thoroughly so they could be used again. This method of cleanliness—washable and reusable cloth—is still in use by girls and women in developing countries.

Also during most of the nineteenth century, almost no women wore their hair short. They let it grow and grow, proud of its length. Those teenage girls who did not have naturally curly hair had to do what Mary did. They used a curling iron to make long curls, which most wore down, but sometimes, particularly for parties, they stacked up on top of their heads. Mary tended to wear her curls down and perched fancy tall hats right on the very top of her head.

Today, there are electric curling irons to turn straight hair into curly hair, but then the iron had to be heated over the fireplace coals or on the cook stove. Mary and her sisters had to be very careful of how hot they got the iron — too much and they would scorch their hair and it would fall out! Too little, and the curls would straighten out in the middle of a party! It's hard to curl your own hair with an iron, so it's probably true that Mrs. Baker was the one who tested the heat of the iron and did the actual winding of the hair around the hot iron for each of her daughters as long as they lived at home.

Until they moved to Sanbornton Bridge, no matter whether the family were going to visit friends, or to church, or to a party, they went in a wagon, not a proper carriage. Mary's oldest sister finally convinced their stubborn father to get a carriage so that they could travel in style pulled by horses—not in a wagon full of straw drawn by oxen.

While the Bakers were still living on the big farm in Bow, they began attending the Congregational church that Mary's mother's family had established. It had an enormous congregation; some 1,000 adults and children came from miles around. The church was in the town of Pembroke across the Merrimack River from Bow. One can imagine what took place early Sunday morning.

Mr. Baker and one or two of the boys would clean the pair of

oxen, put on their harness, and ready the wagon with clean straw and quilts. The girls would get the breakfast ready, then all would change into "Sunday" clothes. Once all were loaded onto the wagon, they drove down the long hill through the fields and orchards to the road alongside the river. They would turn left, and go about four miles to a bridge crossing on the south edge of Concord; then turn right, going about four miles back down the river to Pembroke. That trip, with the slow but steady oxen, could take as long as two hours.

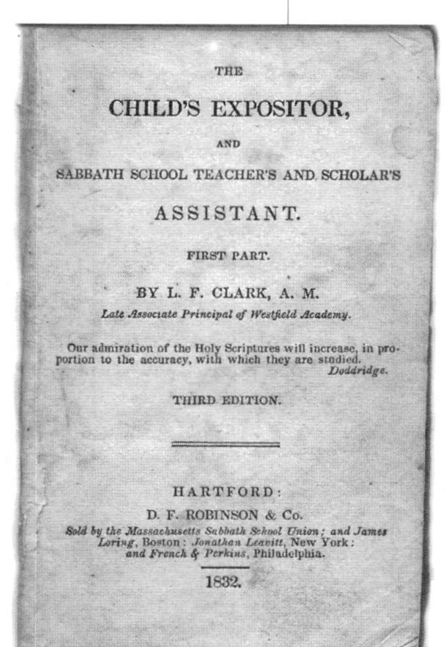

THE

CHILD'S EXPOSITOR,

AND

SABBATH SCHOOL TEACHER'S AND SCHOLAR'S

ASSISTANT.

FIRST PART.

BY L. F. CLARK, A. M.

Late Associate Principal of Westfield Academy.

Our admiration of the Holy Scriptures will increase, in proportion to the accuracy, with which they are studied.

Doddridge.

THIRD EDITION.

HARTFORD:

D. F. ROBINSON & Co.

Sold by the Massachusetts Sabbath School Union; and James Loring, Boston: *Jonathan Leavitt*, New York: *and French & Perkins*, Philadelphia.

1832.

This is an 1832 "Sabbath School" teacher's guide for teaching Sunday school. Something similar probably was used in the Sabbath school where Mary taught.

For the Bakers, under Mark Baker's strict eye, Sunday was a Sabbath day of rest.

Only the minimum of farm chores could be done. No play time at all. A day for worshipping. But, of course, not just for the adults but even more for the children, this was a time to begin and to establish friendships. Mary taught in the Sunday school as well as worshipped with her parents at the several services held throughout the day.

Her pupils loved her, and many of the adults found her devotion to the Bible most remarkable. Yet, from letters saved over the years and kept by the Christian Science Church, it's clear she was popular, too, with fellow teenagers. "Fun," was a word often used to describe her. That was really something special for Mary Baker—to be able to be entirely serious about her church work, and at the same time a delight to other teenagers who were not so devoted to church as she was.

Of course, Mary had to want to have fun with friends and relatives; she had to make the effort to join in their pleasures. And at the same time, she had to find her own time to read, study, and write. Like all discoverers, Mary had to prepare herself to be ready for her discovery.

Thomas Edison, for example, had to spend countless hours in his laboratory testing one metal after another before he could discover one that would burn safely in a glass globe. It took him even longer to discover how to make a battery that could store electricity.

Thomas Alva Edison was born twenty-six years after Mary Baker, and like her discovery, his discoveries are as useful today as they were more than 100 years ago. He never went to college and, like young Mary Baker, never had much formal schooling. Yet Edison is remembered for defining a genius as: "Two percent inspiration and 98 percent perspiration." Mary would certainly agree. Asked what made for successful praying, she answered: "Work, work, work, watch and pray."

Message to The Mother Church for 1902, P. 2.

Isaac Newton, who made his discoveries 200 years before Thomas Edison and Mary Baker, unlike them, was a university graduate, having studied both Greek and mathematics at Cambridge University in England. He not only discovered laws governing gravity and why the moon did not crash into the earth, he also discovered that light was not a single substance but a group of rays of different colors.

He, too, would have agreed with Thomas Edison and Mary

Baker Eddy that failures were important aids to discovery. What was said of Edison was surely true of Eddy and Newton: "Tireless perseverance and long hours of work are the secrets of Edison's success."

For Mary, understanding the Bible was the key to her discovery, and so it was that struggling with her father and the church elders, praying for her own healing from mental stress and physical ills, and coping with the loss of her beloved brother pushed her to ponder ever so deeply how the Old and New Testament healings were accomplished

Scrapbook

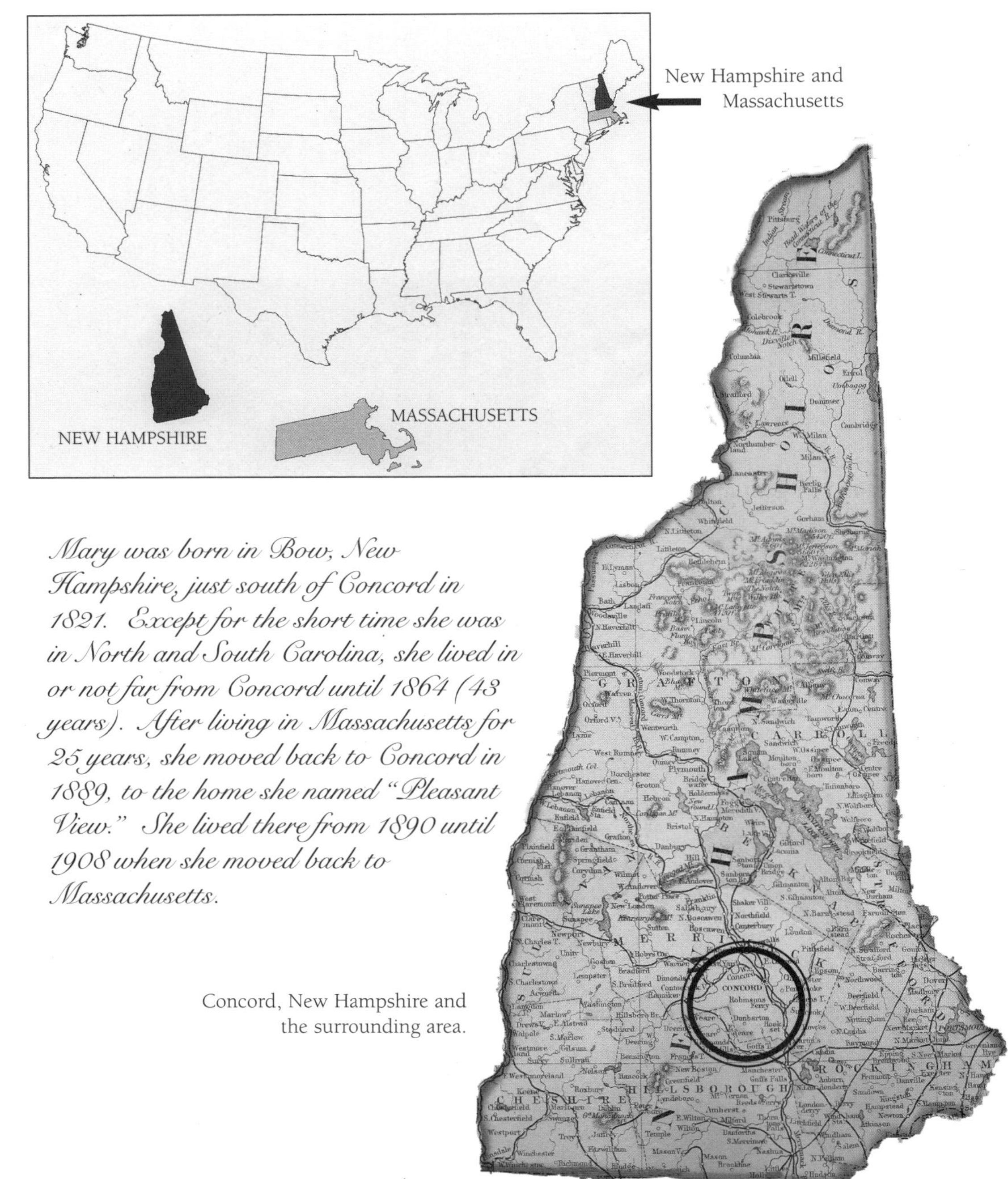

Mary was born in Bow, New Hampshire, just south of Concord in 1821. Except for the short time she was in North and South Carolina, she lived in or not far from Concord until 1864 (43 years). After living in Massachusetts for 25 years, she moved back to Concord in 1889, to the home she named "Pleasant View." She lived there from 1890 until 1908 when she moved back to Massachusetts.

Concord, New Hampshire and the surrounding area.

Danis C. Mutchler

This is a drawing of what the Baker farmhouse might have looked like in 1830. No original photographs of the home, barnyard, or outbuilding have been located.

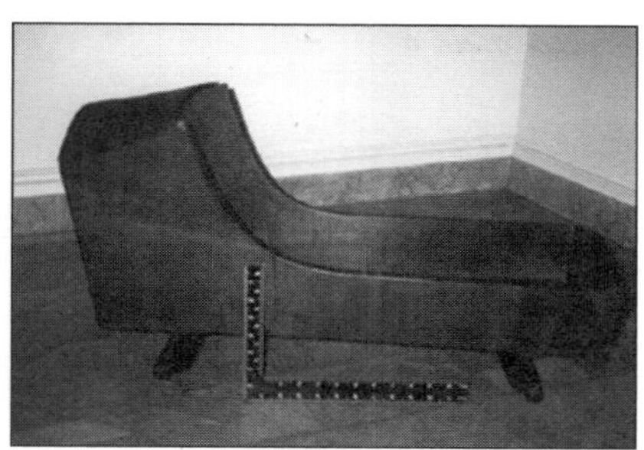

Courtesy of The Longyear Museum

Cradle used one by one, by the Baker children. The metal angle was not in the Baker home in the 1800's, but was placed there in 1999 to show the size.

Courtesy of The Longyear Museum

Baker family Bible and schoolbooks.

Mary's father's desk, his glasses, and items used at the time.

Courtesy of The Longyear Museum

Courtesy of The Longyear Museum

A set of brass andirons that were used in the Baker Farm fireplace to make sure that logs and pitch pine knots had plenty of air underneath.

Phi Beta Kappa catalogue containing notice of Mary's beloved brother Albert's election to this honorary society while at Dartmouth College.

CATALOGUE

OF

THE NEW HAMPSHIRE ALPHA

OF THE

Φ. Β. Κ.

DARTMOUTH COLLEGE,

HANOVER, N. H.

1867.

HANOVER:
PRINTED AT THE DARTMOUTH PRESS.
1867.

C. PARSONS

COURTESY OF THE LONGYEAR MUSEUM

The Woodman-Sanbornton Academy at Sanbornton Square was one of the schools that Mary attended.

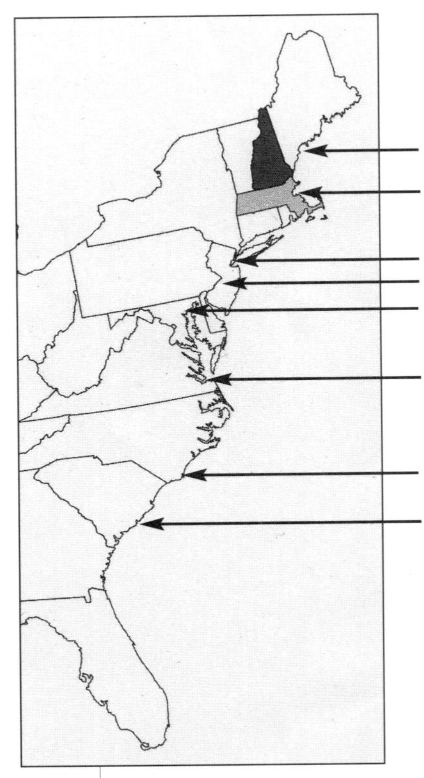

ALICE DE CAPRIO

Drawing of the boat Mary and Wash well might have taken on Christmas Day, 1843, for the long rough sea voyage to Wilmington, North Carolina. The boat would have stopped at the major ports shown on the map.

COURTESY OF THE LONGYEAR MUSEUM

Wash Glover. From a miniature portrait on ivory.

COURTESY OF THE LONGYEAR MUSEUM

Mary Baker Patterson (c. 1850) demonstrating the use of the curling iron. From an original tintype photograph.

COURTESY OF THE LONGYEAR MUSEUM

Mary and her second husband, Daniel Patterson, lived in this house in North Groton, New Hampshire from 1855-1860.

C. Parsons

A picture of Mary (taken about 1851) comforting an infant in a photographer's studio. Mary is wearing a dress she repaired by adding velvet decoration to cover threadbare areas.

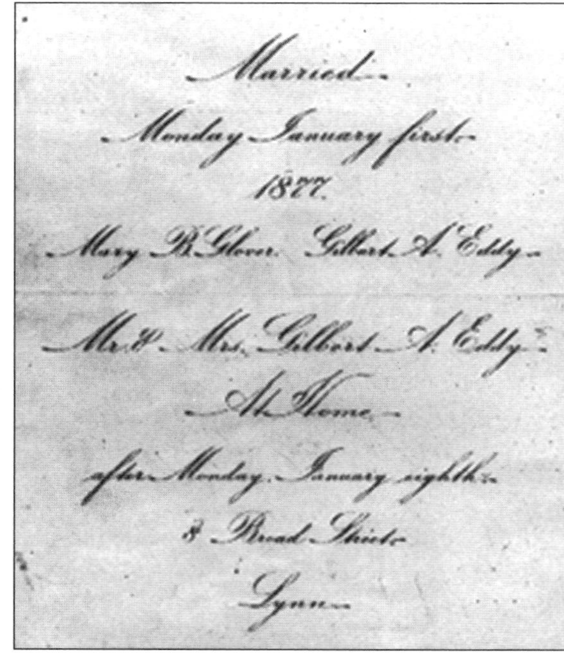

Married

Monday January first

1877.

Mary B. Glover Gilbert A. Eddy

Mr. & Mrs. Gilbert A. Eddy

At Home

after Monday January eighth

8 Broad Street

Lynn

Courtesy of The Longyear Museum

The formal announcement card of Mary and Gilbert Eddy's marriage.

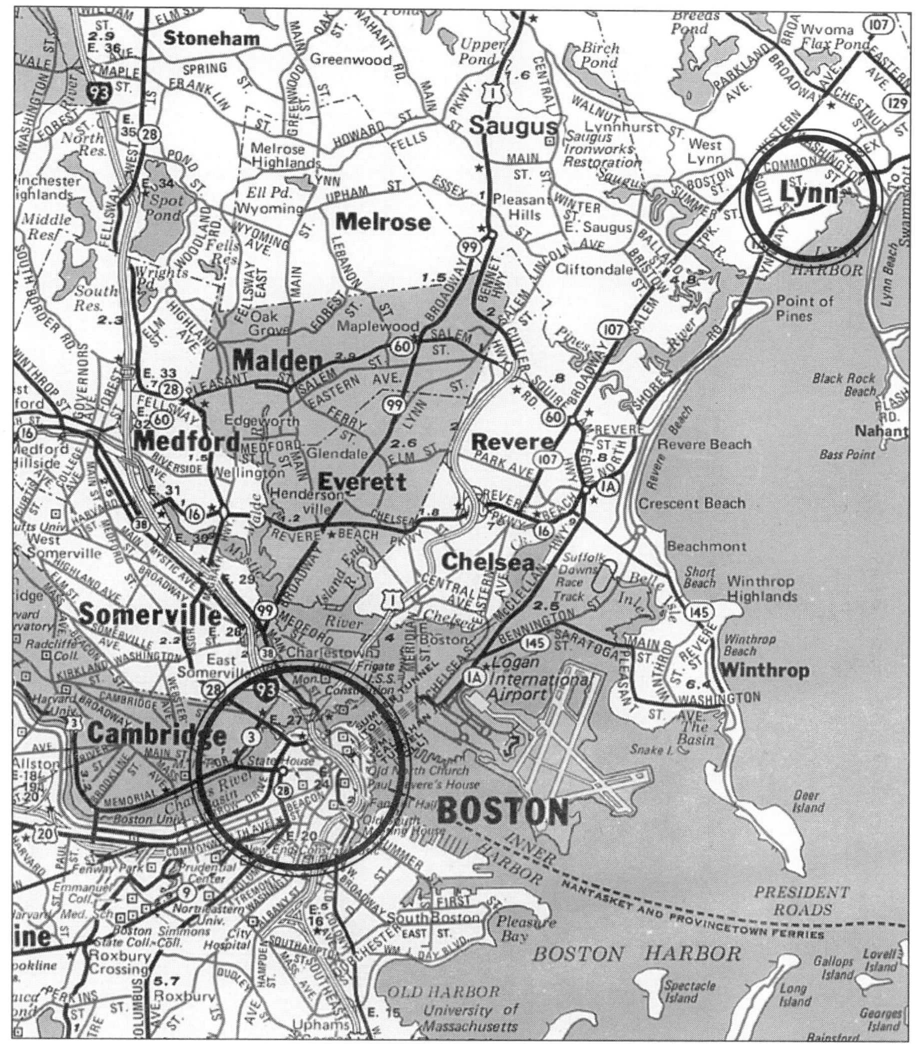

Courtesy of The National Survey, Inc., Chester, Vermont ©2000

Mary and Daniel Patterson moved to Lynn, Massachusetts (just north of Boston) in 1864. Later, when she was married to Gilbert Eddy, they lived in both Lynn and the greater Boston area. Mary Baker Eddy would make Boston the headquarters for the Christian Science Church, and she would live for a short time in the city of Boston.

ECLECTIC PHYSICIAN,

No. 404 I street, between 11th and 12th,

June 21. WASHINGTON, D. C. 4w

MRS. A. E. CUTTER,

HOMEOPATHIC and Mesmeric Physician and Midwife, will take a few patients at her residence for treatment. Persons wishing a quiet place where they can have the best of care, with the advantages of the vapor and other modes of bathing, can address 41 ADDISON STREET, CHELSEA, MASS. Has been very successful in treating cancers, tumors, felons, scarlet fever and measles. 4w*—June 27.

DR. ROUNDY AND WIFE,

CLAIRVOYANT, Magnetic and Electric Physicians, have recently furnished a house on Quincy avenue, in QUINCY, MASS., where they are still Healing the Sick with good success. Board and treatment reasonable. Address, QUINCY, MASS. 4w*—June 6.

ANY PERSON desiring to learn how to heal the sick can receive of the undersigned instruction that will enable them to commence healing on a **principle of science** with a success far beyond any of the present modes. No medicine, electricity, physiology or hygiene required for unparalleled success in the most difficult cases. No pay is required unless this skill is obtained. Address, MRS. MARY B. GLOVER, Amesbury, Mass., Box 61. 12*—June 20.

MRS. MA[illegible] their autograph, or lock of hair, will give psychometrical delineations of character, answer questions, &c. Terms $1.00 and red stamp. Address, MARY LEWIS, Morrison, Whiteside Co., Ill. June 20.—3w*

MRS. M. SMITH, Clairvoyant and Magnetic Physician, will prescribe and give advice by mail. Fee $1.00. Address, Box 1165, Aurora, Ill. 4w*—June 27.

DR. J. T. GILMAN PIKE.

Courtesy of The Longyear Museum

Mary Glover's advertisement that appeared in the "Banner of Light" newspaper July 4, 1868. In it she offered "to teach how to heal the sick without medicine, electricity, physiology, or hygiene, and at no cost unless the pupil obtains the skill."

Historic house on Broad Street in Lynn, Massachusetts, bought by Mary Glover in 1875, and in which she wrote the first edition of "Science and Health." She rented out all but one attic room that was both her office and her bedroom.

Courtesy of The Longyear Museum

Courtesy of The Longyear Museum

Mary Baker Eddy's fountain pen used to write "Miscellaneous Writings" in 1897. The rubber band around the pen kept the ink from staining her fingers.

COURTESY OF THE LONGYEAR MUSEUM

The record book given to Mrs. Eddy recording the names of the Busy Bees—such as Dorothy Baldwin—and listing how much each one had contributed. The First Church of Christ, Scientist used this accounting to determine how much each Busy Bee should receive from the invested funds at age twenty-one.

COURTESY OF THE LONGYEAR MUSEUM

A handcrafted Noah's Ark with the house before the building of the boat deck. It was given by Mrs. Eddy to a neighbor child in Concord, New Hampshire. (c. 1890)

C. Parsons

This top picture is from a post card printed in Frankfurt, Germany in 1900 showing the street-side view of Pleasant View, Mary Baker Eddy's home in Concord, New Hampshire. From the third floor tower room at the back of the house she could see the land in Bow where she was born and lived until she was sixteen.

Visitor's Day at Pleasant View. The guests are behind the stables and the two horses harnessed to the carriage are Princess and Dolly (or Major who replaced Dolly when she died).

Courtesy of The Longyear Museum

Visitors to Pleasant View looking over the hay and rye fields. The photo was taken sometime between 1892 and 1908.

Courtesy of The Longyear Museum

Courtesy of The First Church of Christ, Scientist

The kitchen (flower and herb) garden at Pleasant View.

The boat house and pond at Pleasant View (see Miscellaneous Writings, pp 203-207).

Courtesy of The First Church of Christ, Scientist

Courtesy of The First Church of Christ, Scientist

John Salchow is driving Nelly and Jerry who are pulling the reaper in the Pleasant View twenty acre field of rye wheat. The hired hand frees the reaper blades when caught on a rock or bramble.

COURTESY OF THE LONGYEAR MUSEUM

571 Columbus Avenue, Boston, Massachusetts.

From 1884-1887 this was the site of the Massachusetts Metaphysical College, and the home, for a time, of its founder, president, and instructor, Mary Baker Eddy.

By 1906, "Science and Health" had been through 418 editions (printings), with some changes made in nearly every edition. It was in the 226th edition printed in 1902 that the final chapter entitled "Fruitage" was added. It gives accounts of people who had been healed by reading "Science and Health."

1885 edition of *Science and Health*, page 169.

Ques. What is the scientific statement of being?
Ans. There is no Life, substance, or intelligence in matter; all is Mind, there is no matter. Spirit is immortal Truth, matter is mortal error. Spirit is the real and eternal, matter the unreal and temporal. Spirit is God, and man is His image and likeness; hence, man is spiritual and not material.

Question. — What is the scientific statement of being?
Answer. — There is no life, truth, intelligence, nor substance in matter. All is infinite Mind and its infinite manifestation, for God is All-in-all. Spirit is immortal Truth; matter is mortal error. Spirit is the real and eternal; matter is the unreal and temporal. Spirit is God, and man is His image and likeness. Therefore man is not material; he is spiritual.

Present edition of *Science and Health*.
The Scientific Statement of Being is now found on page 468.

CHAPTER THREE

Husband and Baby

When Mary was ten years old, her oldest brother married one of the Glovers, a family who lived in Concord. Her brother had long since left the Baker farm and was a building contractor in Boston. One of the men working with him was George Washington Glover, and it was George's sister with whom Samuel fell in love.

At the wedding party, Mary, one of the youngest of all the many cousins there, took George's eye, and laughingly he told her that when she grew up he would marry her. She saw him at yet another family wedding party when she was a teenager, and this time they talked and danced together, and began writing letters forth and back.

George Washington Glover served on the staff of the Governor of New Hampshire, and was awarded the title of "Major." To his family and friends he was called "Wash," but professionally he was called Major Glover. In 1839, after learning the building trade in Boston, he moved to Charleston, South Carolina, where he became a partner in a firm as a building contractor. He joined

the Freemasons in Charleston that same year and was a Royal Arch Mason, an officer of St. Andrews Lodge. The Freemasons were then, and are today, a somewhat secret society of men who carry out services for each other and for their communities. Wash Glover was very successful, and although the area had seven building contractors, Glover's firm did some 50 percent of all the building business. Nevertheless, he did get back to New England every few years.

Wash Glover's building firm used slave labor as well as contract laborers. In a tongue-in-cheek letter to his sister, Eliza Ann, and brother-in-law Sam Baker, he told them that if they would name their first son after him, he would give them a slave worth $1,000. Of course, as you can tell, if they did name their son "George," it could be for either uncle, since Samuel's brother also was named George. And while North and South Carolina considered slavery lawful, it was not so in Massachusetts.

In another letter to his sister, written in 1841, Wash Glover assured her that during his recent visit to Boston and Concord he had, ". . . received more solid comfort (he spelled this 'solled cumfut') in April those three days than I have received for the last five years before." It is certainly safe to assume that some of that "solled cumfut" came from spending some time with his bride-to-be, Mary Baker.

A word about spelling in the 1800s. Some grammar books still used British spelling, and a good many school teachers, themselves still high school students, spelled phonetically; that is, by sound. Orthography, or the science of spelling, was still in its infancy in this new Republic. While Mary was a great memorizer, a studious reader, and a fluent writer—she was a terrible speller. In fact, her spelling was of such a poor condition that whatever she wrote for publication—including her popular textbook—had to be corrected by a grammarian.

We can be sure that Mary Baker and Wash Glover had more in common on which to start their marriage than poor spelling, but it must have amused them both to know they shared this difficulty. Not, mind you, that it seems to have stopped them from corresponding, or Mary from sending her writing to newspapers and magazines.

In the summer of 1843, when Mary was twenty-two and George Washington Glover was thirty-three, they became engaged. On December 10, in the Baker's Sanbornton home, filled to the rafters with friends and relatives, they were married.

Because they were to move to the deep south, they spent the next two weeks visiting in Concord and even making a trip to the old Baker farm in Bow—a special treat at Mary's request. On Christmas day they boarded a boat in Boston harbor headed for Wilmington, North Carolina, and had an extremely rough trip down the east coast on the raging Atlantic Ocean.

Wash had traveled several times by boat along this stormy coast, so it was he who provided tender concern and care for Mary, who later reported to her family that she "laid hopelessly sea-sick in the cabin for most of the journey."

Peel, *Mary Baker Eddy: The Years of Discovery*, P. 69.

Wash's business plans were to go to the island of Haiti, where he had a large contract to build a cathedral, and then to return to Charleston, South Carolina, to make his permanent home. Mary, for her part, immediately contacted the editor of a local monthly magazine and was added to the list of contributors advertised as, "The most popular American female writers . . . of this city."

But Mary and her husband spent only a short time in Charleston; Wash had business in Wilmington, North Carolina, and they moved there for the next several months. Yes, Mary immediately began writing for the local paper. The daughter of one of Wash's business contacts said of Mary: "She was extremely beautiful, one of the prettiest young women I have ever seen. I imagine that she was always great for writing verses, for she had no sooner come to Wilmington than she began contributing rhymes to the local paper."

Another woman, recalling a luncheon with Mary Glover described her as "a very beautiful woman, brilliant in conversation, and most gracious in her manner."

Tragedy struck Wash Glover's business. All the building materials he had purchased for the cathedral in Haiti were stolen, and he came down with a fatal case of one of the most dreaded diseases of the day, yellow fever. Mary, pregnant with their child, nursed him, prayed for him, and did whatever she could to see him through this dread disease.

But he died on June 28th, just six months after their wedding. His fellow Masons, recognizing that his pregnant widow was now without husband or income, took up a collection in her behalf. And one of the Masons escorted her back home.

They left Wilmington by train for Weldon, North Carolina, and next by coach to Portsmouth, Virginia. They took a steamboat to Baltimore and the port at Frenchton. From here they took a train across Delaware to New Castle, where they took another boat to Philadelphia and Bristol, Pennsylvania. They changed trains again to Jersey City, where they caught the ferry across the water to New York City.

Mary's brother, Samuel, the one married to her dead husband's sister, met her in New York, and escorted her the rest of the way home. They took a boat to the beautiful horseshoe harbor at Stonington, Connecticut. From there it was the train into Boston, then the train up to Concord, and then from there to Sanbornton Bridge probably in a carriage provided by one of their many Ambrose, Glover, or Baker relatives.

Before she left Wilmington, Mary wrote and had published in the local paper the following short poem:

The Widow's Prayer
by Mary M. Glover

Peel, *Mary Baker Eddy: The Years of Discovery*, P. 77.

For trials past I would not grieve,
  But count my mercies o'er;
And teach the heart Thou hast bereaved
  Thy goodness to adore.

Thou gavest me friends in my distress,
  Like manna from above;
Thy mercy ever I'll confess,
  And own a Father's love.

In a poem written a bit later, titled "Wind of the South," this verse testifies to her distress and deep sense of loss:

O say do worms dare revel round
The casket where no gems can rust?
Hath loveliness a level found
Beneath the cold and common dust?

Peel, *Mary Baker Eddy: The Years of Discovery*, P. 78.

George Washington Glover II arrived on September 12, 1844. It had been a very difficult birth, and a wet nurse had to be found immediately as Mary was too ill to nurse her son. A neighbor woman who had twins, one of whom had died, had sufficient breast milk, so she came to the house several times a day to feed baby George for his first year.

Mahala Sanborn lived in the Baker home to help with the housework, and it was she who nursed bedridden Mary for the next several months. Baby George, as vigorously healthy as his mother was sickly, bonded with Mahala, with whom he spent the majority of his time.

Mary's sisters had babies about the same time. To Martha was born Ellen a few months before Georgy (as his mother called

him); and to Abigail a few months later was born Albert. They lived close enough so that the three cousins often played together. But little Georgy was physically stronger than the other two and had to be disciplined constantly.

As Mary's health improved, she began thinking of what she would do to become independent once again. She had no income; she was a widow with a son to feed and clothe. She was the only one of the six Baker children still living at home.

In 1846, she started a primary school that was modern for its day but proved to require more physical energy than frail Mary had to give. She was then hired as a substitute teacher, working on those days she was in good enough health. She continued writing, but pay for both the teaching and writing were not enough to allow her to move into a home of her own.

Then in 1849 her mother died, and she, Georgy, and her father moved into a smaller house, one with no attached farm land. There is some suggestion that grandfather Mark was very rough with little George, causing Mary acute distress. Mary and Georgy lived there only a year. Then, Mark Baker remarried, and Mary and Georgy moved in with her sister Abigail Tilton, her successful mill-owner husband, and their son Albert.

But boisterous Georgy frightened his Aunt Abigail, and she was concerned about his treatment of her son Albert, a year younger than Mary's son, and himself slight of build. Since her sister Mary was often ill and had no other home—nor any money to rent a place of her own—Abigail persuaded Mary to send Georgy to live with his old nurse, Mahala. Mary reluctantly agreed although Mahala, now married, lived some forty miles away in North Groton, New Hampshire.

This was one low point for Mary: Widowed. Penniless. Bossed by her older sister. Deprived of her only child. On a diet of bread and water. Sickly and frail. She wrote her brother George a sad letter after the 1850 Thanksgiving Day spent with her now widowed sister Martha and her two children, Abigail's family, her father, and her stepmother, part of which states:

"This anniversary has indeed passed—but the absent and the *dead*—where were they? Not with us as we gathered slowly and silently about the table and at evening with deeper memories separated!"

Little did Mary know how few times she would see her son before he was an adult. As usual, her thoughts about the situation turned into poetry. Here is the first verse of one poem she placed in her scrapbook when Georgy moved away:

Go little voyager, o'er life's rough sea —
Born in a tempest! Choose thy pilot God.
The Bible, let thy chart forever be —
Anchor and helm its promises afford. . .

Peel, *Mary Baker Eddy: The Years of Discovery*, P. 98.

That's the discoverer talking. By now, if not much earlier, Mary Baker's chart was the Bible; God was her pilot, her leader, her salvation.

What a difficult eight years between 1843 and 1851:

✣ Happily married.

✣ Thrilled when she discovered she was pregnant.

✣ Horrified when her husband lost his business and then his life.

✣ Distressed that she was unable to care for her newborn son.

✣ Grief-stricken when her beloved mother died.

✣ Disturbed when her father remarried and she had to move out of her home.

✣ Shocked when her sister sent son Georgy forty miles away to live.

✣ Annoyed that her prayers did not free her from her restrictive diet.

As a help to readers, here's an explanation of the names under which Mary Baker was known throughout the years:

Miscellaneous Writings, Preface P. x.

From 1821-1842, Mary Baker
From 1843-1852, Mary Glover
From 1853-1866, Mary Baker Patterson
From 1867-1876, Mary Baker Glover
From 1877, Mary Baker Eddy

CHAPTER FOUR

Poverty and Sickness

After Georgy moved away, Mary Glover spent the next eighteen months sick in bed. Sister Abigail Tilton's home was well equipped, and servants were hired to take care of the housework, cooking, care of Abigail's son, and to provide Mary with her special Graham's diet. Sometimes she added a cooked weak cereal to the bread and water diet.

When Mary was up and about, she was always sought after as a bright conversationalist—full of fun, clever with words, pretty, and dignified. When she had to go to a dentist for some serious work on her teeth, she was attended to by a Dr. Daniel Patterson, who was also a student of homeopathy, a medical treatment that uses natural herbs.

Mary seriously explored this type of treatment of disease for herself and others. As you will remember, Mary was the one on the Baker farm who healed the farm animals. And even in her sickest days, she roused herself to think of ways to heal others when they were brought to her.

While she was living with her sister, a dear friend of the family was suffering from a disease called "dropsy," which today is known as edema. Fluids accumulate in parts of the body and cause tumors. The physician gave up the case and the friend turned to Mary, who began prescribing the same drugs as the doctor had prescribed. Mary was pretty sure it was not the drugs, but her prayers that would make the difference. Yet her patient wanted the drugs.

So, Mary, kept prescribing the drugs, gradually adding water to the solution until no drug was left. The patient was healed. Recalling this healing, after her discovery of Christian Science, Mary Baker Eddy told one of her fellow Christian Scientists that this was "a falling apple to me. It made plain to me that mind governed the whole question of her recovery." Then continuing with how she prayed for herself so that she could be a healer she said, "I was always praying to be kept from sin, and I waited and prayed for God to direct me."

Peel, *Mary Baker Eddy: The Years of Discovery*, P. 136.

That "falling apple" is a reference to the discoverer Isaac Newton who, when an apple dropped out of a tree onto the top of his head, began figuring out what caused all things to fall to earth; he named it the law of gravity.

Dr. Patterson, Mary's dentist, didn't do a proper job on her teeth at her first visit, so she had to return several more times. He fell in love with Mary's eyes! And with Mary. Dr. Patterson wore very fancy clothes even in his dentist's office: a formal dark suit, a handsome frilled shirt, a colorful necktie, and he never went out without wearing a top hat and soft leather gloves.

Bit by bit, Mary began thinking that perhaps this man who

kept asking her to marry him was telling her the truth; that he really would accept little Georgy into their home, and that his dental business would take care of them financially.

Years later, this is what Mary wrote about the fact that Dr. Patterson not only lied about making a home for her son, but also about his business sense. And also Mary wrote, he was unfaithful to the marriage:

> *My second marriage was very unfortunate, and from it I was compelled to ask for a bill of divorce. . .*
>
> *My dominant thought in marrying again was to get back my child, but after our marriage his stepfather was not willing he should have a home with me. A plot was consummated for keeping us apart. The family to whose care he was committed very soon removed to what was then regarded as the Far West.*
>
> *After his removal a letter was read to my little son, informing him that his mother was dead and buried.*

Retrospection and Introspection, P. 20.

When Mary and Dr. Patterson married, they moved to a very small village in New Hampshire named North Groton. Patterson borrowed money from Mary's sisters to rent a house and some forest land, and to operate a saw mill as well as continue his dental work. He not only made house calls as a dentist, but he sometimes went away for weeks at a time, leaving Mary in a rented house with no heat but a fireplace, and no man about to take care of the firewood, the horse, or the cow.

Even before little Georgy was taken away from New England, his mother had no way to get from that little house on the side of the stream that powered the saw mill, to the town of Franklin some twenty miles away where he was living. For at least six if not eight of the winter months, the little house was in shadow: that is, it was in the deepest, snowiest, and coldest spot possible. When Mary Patterson lived there, there was both a church (since collapsed and not replaced) and a one-room schoolhouse, which is still standing.

Mary often went to the school about one-third of a mile from her house to volunteer and help with the children's lessons when she was feeling well enough to do so. One of the village women, who was blind, came every day to visit Mrs. Patterson and listen to her read; also to carry out any little chores she could do.

The house the Pattersons rented is still standing by the side of the stream, and close by are wild strawberry plants. They must have been there when Mary Patterson was living there, and it seems reasonable to imagine her little blind friend helping Mary pick and prepare these delicious little berries. Wild strawberries are tiny, and have a much sweeter and stronger flavor than the cultivated berries we buy today in stores, or even from roadside stands. It's also reasonable to assume that Mrs. Patterson and her helper hulled the berries and then cooked them on the top of the woodstove to make jam.

Dr. Patterson squandered whatever money he made fixing and cleaning teeth. He was neither a good woodsman nor a reliable mill worker, as it takes considerable skill to turn a tree into lumber suitable for house-building and flooring. He declared bankruptcy; that is, he lost the right to cut trees on the woodlot he had rented, and because he had not paid the rent on the house or the mill, he lost the right to use the mill, and a short time after that was forced to move out of the house. All their furniture was sold to pay some of the bills.

Mary and her husband moved about ten miles north to a house in Rumney, New Hampshire, in which they rented three rooms. Later, they rented a six-room house nearby. His dental office area was unheated, and the only one of the three rooms with heat—from a fireplace—was the parlor where Mary spent time tutoring village children and writing the poems she sold for pennies to local newspapers.

Their bedroom, unheated, was above the parlor. To go to the bathroom, they had to use a privy outside whatever the weather.

Mary continued to offer healing to those who came to her. One case, in particular, she told to a friend many years later:

> *Mrs. Smith . . . came to me with her infant, whose eyes were diseased, a mass of inflammation, neither pupil nor iris discernable. I gave the infant no drugs, held her in my arms a few moments while lifting my thoughts to God, then returned the babe to her mother healed. In grateful memory thereof Mrs. Smith named her babe, "Mary," and embroidered a petticoat for me.*

Fettweis and Warneck, *Mary Baker Eddy: Christian Healer*, P. 22.

But Mary was not satisfied just to heal, she wanted to know *how* she did it, and especially how Jesus and his disciples had done it. She knew God was the key. When asked years later, when the whole world was reading about her discovery, which of the Ten Commandments was her favorite, she answered without hesitation that it was the first:

THOU SHALT HAVE NO OTHER GODS BEFORE ME.

The Ten Commandments can be found in Exodus, the second book of the Bible. They are in chapter twenty, verses one through seventeen.

But this young "motherless" mother had yet to make her discovery; in fact, Mary was faced with years and years of struggle and success, then more struggle, before she was able to tell the world what she had discovered and how they could use her discovery to be healers themselves. Her pre-discovery work in her isolated village laboratories was to find a way, as she explained it: ". . .to trace all physical effects to a mental cause."

The Civil War began while the Pattersons were in Rumney. Dr. Patterson went to the front lines on a mission for a New Hampshire official and was captured by the Rebel forces. On April 2, 1862, he wrote a letter from his Richmond, Virginia, prison to his wife in Rumney, New Hampshire. In it he said, "You will be amazed to learn that I am in prison."

Right away Mary began writing a barrage of letters to officials in both government offices and in the Union Army. Her next letter from her husband told not of his rescue, but of the fact he had been taken from the fairly decent Richmond prison and had been placed in a much worse facility in Salisbury, North Carolina.

The prisoners were kept in tents on a barren field, and when Dr. Patterson refused to sign a paper saying he would not try to escape, he was put into an underground cave. Nevertheless, eventually, he did escape.

When Mary wrote her husband's brother to tell him she had been unsuccessful in getting her husband released from prison, she ended the letter: "Your desolate sister, Mary M. Patterson."

Incredible as it seems, about this same time, Mary's long-lost son, George Washington Glover II, also wrote to his mother. At age sixteen Georgy had run away from home, lied to the Union Army officials saying that he was seventeen, and was accepted. One of the Union Army volunteers, who offered to write letters for his fellow soldiers, was able to trace George Glover's birth and discovered that his mother was not dead.

When she got that first letter, she wept with joy, and immediately began writing to him. A year later he was wounded and hospitalized, and she prayed for him. When he was out of the hospital, she hoped he would come to visit her in New England, but he reenlisted. Again, she turned to poetry to help her.

How these sad eyes dim with weeping
Long to gaze upon my son;
Gazing back upon his childhood,
Wishing more I could have done.

Peel, *Mary Baker Eddy: The Years of Discovery*, P. 177.

Her husband's imprisonment and the emotional reaction on hearing from her son took a heavy toll on Mary's fragile health. She wanted to try a cure that involved hypnotism offered by a man named Quimby in Portland, Maine, but she had no way to get there, so she chose instead to go to the Hydropathic Institute in Hill, New Hampshire.

The institute offered some kind of water cure. She found a suitable boarding house and began the treatment, which consisted of baths, rest, a simple diet, and much drinking of water. She got worse instead of better. One of the women she met there had been to Portland, Maine, to take a cure with Quimby, and her enthusiasm for his method made Mary eager to try that next.

She wrote to Quimby telling him that she "had been sick six years with spinal inflammation." She also wrote him about her gastric and bilious attacks and asked him if he would come to Rumney to give her his cure, which she knew only a little about, but she knew did consist of hypnotizing her and rubbing her head with his hands. He wrote back that he could not come to Rumney, but if she would come to Portland, he would see her and decide whether he would be able to heal her.

She appealed for help from one of her brothers, who came to Rumney with a horse-drawn carriage and took her first to Boston. From there they went together by boat to Portland, and then by coach to Quimby's office building. Her spine was so inflamed and sore that she had to be carried from the coach and up a flight of stairs into Dr. Quimby's office.

She did improve while she was there, but after she got back to Rumney, the pain and sickness returned.

About this time, her husband escaped from the Rebel Army prison and made his way back to Rumney. But he was determined to move to a more populous area where he could spend less time riding a horse long distances in all kinds of weather to make dental house calls. They packed up their very few belongings in 1864 and moved to a rental house in Lynn, Massachusetts, a short train ride from Boston, then a city of some 100,000 people.

Except for the short time that Mary and Wash Glover lived in Wilmington, North Carolina, Mary had always lived on a farm or in a tiny village. This move brought her to a city. Even in 1864 Lynn was considered a suburb of Boston and a center of activity in the shoe-making business. Lynn was incorporated as a town in 1631, and in 1643 it had the first ironworks business in the thirteen Colonies. The first fire engine built in the United States was built in Lynn in 1654. And in 1850, Lynn was incorporated as a city.

Today, Lynn has a population of more than 80,000; back in 1860, the Lynn census recorded 19,083 white males and females, and 226 "free colored" males and females. But instead of making a good home for Mary and developing a financially successful business, it is here that Daniel Patterson abandoned Mary, this time for good, going off with another man's wife.

These were eleven difficult years for Mary Baker Glover Patterson after leaving her sister's comfortable home, and arriving in the town of Lynn. Yet Mary spent the time, sick or well, working hard to understand the Bible, particularly the teachings of Jesus and his remarkable record of healings.

She also experimented with a host of remedies. She explored hypnotism, and spiritualism, and the taking of drugs so diluted that none of their chemical power was still in them, to get some understanding of how much faith was required to change a sick person into a healthy person. She had been given drugs, including morphine, by many of the doctors who attended her as a child and teenager and she didn't want to use mind-altering chemicals.

She explored whether nervous disorders could be healed by changing thoughts from agitated nervousness to calmness. She read hundreds of tracts written by people claiming they had found yet a better way to heal sickness. And she kept on studying her Bible and praying the prayers therein to discover whether she could duplicate what Jesus and his disciples had done.

During these eleven years living in rented houses with an often absent and unfaithful husband, she had a son taken away, had all her worldly goods removed by the courts, and seldom had a day without pain and sickness. So, how did she refer to this time when she wrote her own story about her early years?

> *The loss of material objects of affection sunders*
> *the dominant ties of earth and points to heaven.*

Retrospection and Introspection, P. 31.

What an incredible statement! That word "sunders" means

"breaks," or "separates." Through terrible poverty and sickness and the loss one after the other of her beloved brother, first husband, supportive mother, precious son, and second husband, she believed that this testing time pointed her to heaven. What a woman! She was glad to exchange the "ties of earth" for a better understanding of heaven.

CHAPTER FIVE

Pills or Prayers

ary Patterson was now carrying out enormously important experiments in the healing arts. Actually, she'd been doing so since she was a very little girl. Of course, when she was a youngster, her scientific experiments were of the simplest kind. But when she moved to Lynn, Massachusetts, she was forty-three years old, and had been reading not only several translations of the Bible, and the most thoughtful commentaries on the Bible, but also medical journals and material telling about different medical treatments and experimental healing practices.

She was a very careful reader. She both underlined material she found particularly interesting and wrote notes in the margins, giving her own thoughts about what the author of the material said. She did some of her markings with a quill pen that she dipped in an ink bottle. The archives department in the church she founded has preserved many of the books she read and studied at this time.

Also, she kept her own notebooks and scrapbooks telling about her experiments trying various combinations of healing systems,

not only to bring healing to herself but to those who came to her for healing. She also offered to heal neighborhood children and adults who had serious illnesses.

The town of Lynn was filled mostly with descendants of Europeans who had arrived as early as 1629, and a decade or so later with Puritans fleeing England. Swampscott, which became a separate town from Lynn in 1852, was even in those early years a resort town. Hence, in the winter months, rooms could be rented cheaply, and the Pattersons rented rooms in both Lynn and Swampscott. About one hundred years before Mary Patterson moved to Lynn, the shops were producing 400,000 pairs of shoes annually. For fifty years—from 1870 through 1920—Lynn was known as the shoe-production capital of the United States. Mary Patterson's first patients were workers in the local shoe industry.

She had long been trying several diets, and most often held to her bread-and-water-once-a-day meal. But in the interest of her desire to discover how to heal the sick, she tried all kinds of diets and not only took all kinds of pills, but also gave pills to those who were her patients.

Nevertheless, she grew to have no faith in any pills, whether made from natural herbs or from chemicals. She became, through her experimental failures and successes, more and more convinced that the healing had to come from thinking and not from chemistry.

Today, what is often called "massage therapy," was known 100 years ago as "the laying on of hands." Many of those who "doctored" patients by trying to convince them they were well through

thought processes, also gave them back and head rubs, arguing that such "laying on of hands" would help the patient relax, drive out some of the distress and fear, and so help the patient think of herself (or himself) as well.

Mesmerism—often called animal magnetism—also was used to "doctor" sick people. During the time Mary Patterson was searching for cures, mesmerists were gaining popularity. For example, in 1864, it was claimed that there were more than 200 mesmerizers in Boston and throughout New England twenty or thirty lecturers who not only explained how mesmerism worked but also demonstrated it, usually by hypnotising a member of the audience from a stage in a local opera house.

You will remember it was to a man named Dr. Phineas Quimby of Portland, Maine, that Mary Patterson had her brother take her when her spine was unbelievably painful and crippled her so she could not walk.

Quimby mesmerized his patients in order to "feel the patient's pain." That is, Quimby would take on some of the same symptoms that were causing the pain or disease for the patient. First, the patient would feel better, then Quimby would relieve himself of the disease. As Quimby grew more and more confident about his abilities as a mesmerizer, his faith in drugs grew less and less.

Quimby, and many other healing mesmerists, believed that it was some fearful or anxious thought that disturbed the fluids in a person's body, and that doctoring the fluids was not as health-giving as changing the thought, which would "undisturb" the fluids and the patient would get well.

All this was quite in line with the direction of Mary Patterson's scientific experiments. She was giving more thought to God as a healer than most other alternative medicine explorers, yet, like other experimental scientists, she explored all positive systems.

Many of the healers believed that they had some kind of personal positive "electric" power, and that by stroking a patient's body (maybe an injured leg or a disturbed stomach), the positive electricity would flow from the healer to the patient, neutralizing the negative "electricity" in the patient. Many of these spiritualists or mesmerizers also included water in their treatments. Patients were asked to drink water at the moment that the healer was thinking of them, or the healer dipped his hands in water before stroking the patient.

And if a patient believed in the power of a pill, some healers, even if they did not believe in the pills, would let the patients take them, arguing that since it was the patient's thought that would effect the healing, whatever helped turn that thought in a positive direction was all to the good.

This was certainly true for Mary Patterson. She claimed she felt healing in her body after she was carried into Quimby's waiting room and before he had come to talk with her. She found Quimby's mesmeric cure so powerful that after a week's treatments from him, she climbed, unaided, a flight of 182 steps to the dome at the top of the Portland City Hall.

Was this, she asked herself, the way Jesus healed? Was this the Christ (the healing agent told about in the Bible) that she had been trying to find and failed when she prayed for herself, her brother Albert, her husband Wash Glover, her mother, and so many others who had come to her for healing?

On January 10, 1864, Mrs. Patterson gave a public talk to the Portland, Maine, Spiritual Association in that city's Mechanics Hall that was covered by the local press. The report stated, in part: "Having been cured of a disease by Dr. Quimby, Mrs. Patterson alluded in the course of her remarks to the nature of the ills flesh is heir to, and endeavored to explain the cause of such diseases upon metaphysical, physiological, and philosophical principles, but she reasoned so high above the ordinary plane upon which we stood that we failed to comprehend her meaning."

The report continued quoting Mrs. Patterson as saying that "disease is an error of the spirit, and it only needs Truth to combat it."

This business of her speaking "so high above the ordinary plane" was a serious problem for the discoverer, Mary Baker Eddy. Her early schooling in the classics, and her brilliant mind and extensive vocabulary, were, at first, a hindrance to her when she tried to explain her thoughts about mental healing. She devoted years to making the meaning of her discovery clear to everyone, even to those who were not scholars.

After her cure, she continued to visit Quimby's office for the next three months to try to learn how he did the healing work.

She interviewed his patients before they saw him, interviewed them after treatment, and interviewed Quimby about what he thought had happened. She was excited. Was it possible she was making the final discovery?

But to her distress, the relief from her own pain did not last long. Once again, Mary was in pain, crippled, and often bedridden. She continued to write to Quimby and asked him to think healing thoughts about her; but at the same time, she explored with yet more vigor just what it was in the Bible that made possible the healings of every sort of illness.

Over and over Mary Patterson made a solemn promise to God that if God would give her health, she would devote her life to the healing of the sick. And all during this period of seeking a cure for her illnesses, she went regularly to church. It was the custom in many Congregational churches for members of the congregation to stand, when invited, and share a prayer or thought. One of the women who went to the North Groton Congregational Church told one of Mary's biographers:

"Mrs. Patterson frequently responded to the call to offer prayer in public, and her prayers were long remembered as uplifting and helpful." Another who knew her then said, "Prayer, meditation, eager and puzzled interrogation of the Bible, had claimed from childhood much of her energy. . . ."

When her husband escaped from the Confederate Army prison, he went to Sanbornton Bridge to Mary's sister's home, and Mary came from Portland to be with him there. Dr. Patterson was, of course, suffering from the awful conditions of the prison as well as the very difficult time he had going from North Carolina to New Hampshire. He needed the comforts the Tilton home provided.

While there, Mary learned that her sister's son, Albert, was smoking and drinking to alarming excess, and persuaded Abigail to take him to Portland to be cured by Quimby. Albert lost the cravings while he was with Quimby, but got them back again when he returned home. His aunt Mary decided to try to use Quimby's methods to heal him, and discovered that she took on the cravings instead of casting them off altogether.

So, she wrote Quimby to ask him to rid herself of her nephew's addictions, and added in the letter that she was once again suffering from ". . . pain in the back, bilious stomach, and a cold." He wrote back that he had too many patients, and so she prayed for both her nephew and herself. She healed herself of a craving for tobacco and liquor, but her nephew would respond to her prayers only for a time, and then give in to the addictions.

She worked hard to discover whether there was a science underlying Quimby's healing method. She suspected that there was, but he was unable to tell her what it was. She did claim, long after she had discovered Christian Science that: "Dr. Quimby [was] the most progressive, magnetic doctor I ever knew. . ."

But what she wrote and circulated privately about her thinking then in 1864 was radically different from what she wrote after her discovery in 1866. And what she wrote later was refined and

restated after many years of scientific research. In 1908, in one of her church's magazines, she explained:

> *The best mathematician has not attained the full understanding of the principle thereof, in his earliest studies or discoveries. Hence, it were wise to accept only my teachings that I know to be correct. . . .*

The First Church of Christ Scientist and Miscellany, P. 237.

This was true, for example, for the brilliant English mathematician, Isaac Newton, who studied thirty-nine years before he felt he had a full understanding of calculus. His early discovery took place in 1687, and his final writings, known as *Principia*, did not appear until 1726.

Albert Einstein had enormous respect for the work of Isaac Newton and said of him that he was: "An experimenter, theorist, mechanic, and artist. He stands before us strong, certain, and alone." There are many students of Christian Science who would say exactly the same about its discoverer. While Einstein was not a member of the Christian Science Church, he did read the writings of Mary Baker Eddy.

I want to know the thoughts of God. All the rest are details.

Albert Einstein

As noted in Chapter One, as a school child Mary read and studied an essay about the "folly and misery of idleness" by the great Scots writer, Dr. Hugh Blair. He started his essay by stating: "I hope to prove that the idle man, first, shuts the door against all improvement; next, that he opens it wide to every destructive folly; and, lastly, that he excludes himself from the true enjoyment of pleasure."

The following are some of the statements Mrs. Eddy made about idleness after her discovery of Christian Science.

Idleness is the foe of progress.

Miscellaneous Writings, P. 206.

All successful individuals have become such by hard work . . . they spend no time in sheer idleness.

Ibid, P. 230.

If at present [we are] content with idleness, we must become dissatisfied with it.

Science and Health, P. 240.

Mrs. Eddy was not the first spiritual leader to recognize the motherhood of God. In her use of capital letters, however, she was one of the first to speak of God as Mother, as found in this poem, which she said she wrote for "the little children."

Father-Mother God,
Loving me, —
Guard me when I sleep;
Guide my little feet
Up to Thee.

Poems, P. 69.

CHAPTER SIX

Discovery and Direction

Thomas Alva Edison was born in 1847, when Mary Glover was twenty-six. Like Mary, he was home schooled and never went to college. It was electrical force that fascinated him, and his many experiments led to several discoveries.

It was Isaac Newton who said that: "Knowledge is an accumulation of vision of the present added to that of the past."

Newton, Edison, and Eddy had their visions, did their experiments, wrote about what they observed, and positioned themselves to make remarkable discoveries. Edison was able—through his discoveries of what electrical force was and what it could do—to invent the radio, the microphone, the telephone transmitter, the phonograph, the dynamo, and, most importantly, the electric light.

When Edison died, President of the United States Herbert Hoover suggested that at the same moment—for one minute—on the night of October 21, 1931, everyone across the country should turn off all electric lights. This was done by municipal authorities in city after city as well as in most homes. What a dramatic way to show how important Edison's discovery was for not just the United States, but the whole world!

Edison explained to a questioner: "I never did anything worth doing by accident. They came by work." We can suppose he was asked if he had "stumbled" onto his discovery of how to put electric power inside a glass globe. As for that particular discovery Edison said, "I consolidated 3,000 theories."

While young Thomas Edison was exploring electrical power, Mary Baker was exploring spiritual power. As you will recall from her disagreement with her father and the pastor of the church she joined when she was a teenager, she was sure God was a loving God, a good spiritual power, available to everyone regardless of whether they were or were not members of a church. Like Edison, who wanted to harness electrical force, Mary wanted to know how to use spiritual force for healing and direction.

Nicolaus Copernicus, born in 1473, was a Polish astronomer. He, too, worked and worked and worked, studying the motions of what he called "heavenly bodies"—what we call the stars, planets, sun, and moon. Like Isaac Newton, who spent thirty-nine years editing and revising his major work on mathematics, *Principia*, Copernicus first stated his discovery about the movement of the "heavenly bodies" in 1512, but did not feel his book was complete and correct until 1543, some twenty-one years later. Its title was *Concerning the Revolutions of the Heavenly Spheres.*

It was Ptolemy, a Greek astronomer who lived in the second century who insisted that the earth was the center of the universe.

And it was Copernicus who said it wasn't, thirteen centuries later! You can believe it took a lot of thoughtful writing and lecturing for Copernicus to persuade any scientists that the earth went around the sun, and not the other way around.

Ptolemy, and millions of people for hundreds of years, were certainly right that it looked from earth as though the sun moved around the back side of the earth at night and came up in the east and went down in the west on another revolution. What a job Copernicus had to convince not only astronomers and scientists, but also the whole human population of the world to believe him!

Mary Baker Eddy's discovery was metaphysical. She declared that matter—material force—has no real life or substance or intelligence. This was, for most people, even more startling than what Copernicus had discovered. While today a great many people believe the truth of her discovery, most still do not. Mrs. Eddy, in a pamphlet she wrote in 1891, *No and Yes*, compared her discovery with that of Copernicus:

> *The evidence that the earth is motionless and the sun revolves around our planet, is as sensible and real as the evidence for disease; but Science determines the evidence in both cases to be unreal. . . . Copernicus has shown that what appears real, to material sense and feeling, is absolutely unreal. Astronomy, optics, acoustics, and hydraulics are all at war with the testimony of the physical senses. This fact intimates that the laws of Science are mental, not material; and Christian Science demonstrates this.*

No and Yes, P. 6.

Another famous discoverer, Jean Louis Rodolphe Agassiz, was born in Switzerland in 1807—making him fourteen years older than Mary Baker. He became an American citizen in 1862. Unlike Mary Baker and Thomas Edison, he went to the best schools in Europe, and at the age of twenty-three had earned the highest academic degree, Doctor of Philosophy. One of the first books he published (in 1840) was titled, *Studies of the Glaciers*.

Twenty years later he was lecturing at Harvard University and, in 1863, published his most famous work, *Methods of Study in Natural History*. It was one of the books Mrs. Eddy read, reread, and marked up with her notations.

She quotes from Agassiz's book in her book, *Science and Health*, but disagrees with him based on her metaphysical discovery.

Agassiz, she wrote, ". . .forsakes Spirit as the divine origin of creative Truth. . . [and believes] in the material origin of man, for he virtually affirms that the germ of humanity is in a circumscribed and non-intelligent egg." Then she poses the question: "If this be so, whence cometh Life, or Mind, to the human race?"

Mrs. Eddy then continues with a definite statement, a piece of her discovery:

"God is the Life, or intelligence, which forms and preserves the individuality and identity of animals as well as men." This was radical thinking, indeed.

Science and Health, P. 550.

She had spent more than forty years exploring the problem of whether it was material force or spiritual force that controls the universe, including its tiniest insects and its most progressive species, us humans.

Mrs. Eddy dates her moment of discovery as 1866. This is what happened that year.

Quimby, the doctor she went to in Portland, Maine, became seriously ill in 1865 and died in January 1866, causing Mary to study the Bible even more than she had done previously. If there was no science behind the work of Quimby, was there a science behind Jesus' ministry? How could she heal as Jesus did? What was it she needed to understand?

Her father, Mark Baker, died in 1865. He left his home and all his possessions to his son George and, spitefully, left but one dollar to each of his three daughters—Abigail, Martha, and Mary. It was true that Mary's older sisters had good homes and husbands who provided well for them, but Mary was close to homeless and married at that time to a man who continued to be unfaithful and who was constantly in debt. She certainly could have used more than a dollar!

In the winter of 1866, Mary lived in rented, second-floor rooms in Swampscott, the next town north of Lynn. One evening in February, walking with some lady friends from Lynn to Swampscott, Mary Patterson slipped on some ice and crashed to the ground. She was knocked unconscious and was very badly hurt. The people living in the nearest house let her stay there in Lynn overnight, but when she was conscious the next morning, she insisted she be taken to her rented bedroom in Swampscott.

The doctor on the case gave her some morphine to relieve the pain, and this put her to sleep for hours and hours.

She experienced convulsions and had a concussion, and perhaps a fracture of the spine. So serious was her condition that the minister of the Congregational church she attended came to pray with her what is often called "the last rites," a prayer to ease her thought about her upcoming death.

While she was awake, four days after the fall, she asked to be left alone with her Bible. As she explained to her friends and pastor then, and later to those who believed in her discovery, she realized that the following was not just a nice statement made by Jesus, but the truth about her—really about everyone:

"I am the way, the truth, and the life: no man cometh unto the Father but by me."

John 14: 6

In her book, *Science and Health*, Mary Baker Eddy tells what it was she discovered at the moment she thought about that statement by Jesus. Four ideas so convinced her of their truthfulness that she got right out of bed, dressed herself, and walked into the next room to rejoice with her fellow church members about her healing.

She summarizes those four parts of her discovery by stating that ". . .Mind is All and matter is naught. . . ." "Naught" is another word for "zero" or "nothing." And the "Mind" she says is "All," has a capital "M" because it is another name (or a synonym) for God.

Science and Health, Pp. 108-109.

She also explains her discovery in four propositions on page 113 of *Science and Health*, all four of which can be reversed and

still be true. Undoubtedly she studied these sorts of propositions with her brother Albert when she was tutored by him.

"1. *God is All-in-all.*"
[All-in-all is God.]
"2. *God is good. Good is Mind.*"
[Good is God. Mind is good.]
"3. *God, Spirit, being all, nothing is matter.*"
[Matter is nothing, all being God, Spirit.]
"4. *Life, God, omnipotent good, deny death, evil, sin, disease. — Disease, sin, evil, death, deny good, omnipotent God, Life.*"

Her discovery was as radical as could be. Her doctor and her church friends considered her healing a miracle and not the result of understanding some correct spiritual ideas.

Writing about this experience sometime later she explained,

When . . . I was delivered from the dark shadow and portal of death, my friends were frightened at beholding me restored to health.

A dear old lady asked me, "How is it that you are restored to us? Has Christ come again on earth?"

"Christ never left," I replied; "Christ is Truth, and Truth is always here. . . ."

Miscellaneous Writings, P. 180.

Mary had a relapse a few days later and thought she should ask one of Quimby's students to pray for her. He refused, and even suggested that hypnotism and mesmerism were not true healing agents. And so, Mary once again turned to her Bible for inspiration and was once again free from the effects of her fall on the ice.

Several years later, when she was asked why she named the Science she discovered, "Christian Science," she said, ". . . because it is compassionate, helpful, and spiritual."

Retrospection and Introspection, P. 25.

What to do now? What direction to take?

She had to understand more. One way to do this was to try healing others and to teach others how to heal using her discovery. And another, of course, for this woman who had been writing from the first moment she could hold a pen, was to write a pamphlet explaining not just what her discovery was, but how anyone could use it to heal as Jesus had.

She shared what she was writing and thinking with anyone who would listen. Dr. Patterson was not one of them. He had left for good this time, and shortly stopped giving her any money to pay for food or housing. So she moved from house to house, sometimes staying in a room in a boardinghouse and taking meals with other boarders. To pay the rent, she tutored and sewed, and even, in some cases, was paid for the healings she accomplished through her prayers.

When she told her sister about her discovery that "Mind is All and matter is naught," Abigail was horrified. She offered to build Mary a small house on her property, and to provide her with a living allowance if she would give up all this radical talk, but that if she persisted in writing and circulating her "Christian Science" tracts, she would not even send her the money she had been giving her to fill in for Dr. Patterson, her neglectful husband.

Mary refused to stop exploring her discovery, refused to stop telling others about it—and so had to live for the next several years in virtual poverty. She dropped Patterson's name, and was known during the next few years as Mary Glover. And bit by bit she was learning how to apply her spiritual discoveries—healing herself and others. She was able to heal even the most difficult diseases and was able to coach others how to heal using her writings about what God is, what the Christ is, and what the Christ does.

Much of the Christian world at this time believed that Jesus was God. No, no, no, said Mary Glover. In 1870, four years after healing herself from the result of the fall on the ice, she published what she called a "class-book." She stated her discovery in a series of questions and answers:

"*Question.* — What is God?

Science and Health, P. 465.

"*Answer.* — God is incorporeal, divine, supreme, infinite Mind, Spirit, Soul, Principle, Life, Truth, Love."

"Incorporeal" means without a material body. "Infinite" means without beginning or ending.

Later in the class-book, she answered the question, "What is man?" beginning with this startling statement:

"Man is not matter; he is not made up of brain, blood, bones, and other material elements."

You can see why her sister wanted her to stop writing and saying such unpopular things.

But Mary Glover was healed thinking these things. She ate regular balanced meals instead of one meal a day of bread and water; she no longer spent days and weeks helpless in bed unable to move because of a damaged spine; she no longer suffered continuously from convulsions and nervous spasms.

She healed a man named James Ingham of a disease called consumption. He wrote about his healing:

> *I was suffering from pulmonary difficulties, pain in the chest, a hard and unremitting cough, hectic fever, and all those fearful symptoms that made my case alarming. When I first saw Mrs. Glover, I was reduced to such a state of debility as to be unable to walk any distance, or to sit up but a portion of the day; to walk upstairs gave me great suffering from breath. I had not received her attention but a short time, when my bad symptoms disappeared, and I regained health. . . . Her cures are not the result of medicine, mediumship, or mesmerism, but the application of a Principle that she understands.*

In the first edition of *Science and Health,* P. 338.

Mary Glover, while delighted that her experiments using her discovery were often successful, wanted to do more for the world. She wanted the world to understand the "Principle" James Ingham wrote about.

It was extremely rare for anyone in that day to offer healing that didn't include medicine of some kind, or hypnotism, or special diets, or laying on of hands. Mary had tried and discarded all those methods. She now offered her patients only pure prayer based on the fact that "Mind is All and matter is naught."

Not long after the healing of James Ingham of consumption, Mary healed the poet, John Greenleaf Whittier (1807-1892), of the same disease. Whittier is the author of the famous poem, "Snow-Bound." Like Mary, he was born on a New England farm and had little formal schooling. And, like Mary, he wrote about his distaste of slavery. He was sixty-one when Mary Glover healed him of consumption, and he lived twenty-four more years. *The Christian Science Hymnal* contains several of his poems.

Pulpit and Press, P. 54.

One of Whittier's most famous poems, written in 1870, begins: "Dear Lord and Father of us all, / Forgive our foolish ways. . ." It is included in many Protestant hymnals. Another hymn which he entitled "The Healer," was in the first hymnal published by the Christian Science Church and was written after he was healed by Mrs. Eddy. It is on page ninty-six of the current (1932) edition of *The Christian Science Hymnal*.

He stood of old, the holy Christ,
  Amid the suffering throng,
With whom his lightest touch sufficed
  To make the weakest strong.
That healing gift God gives to them

Who use it in His name;
The power that filled the garment's hem
Is evermore the same.

So shalt thou be with power endued
Like him who went about
The Syrian hillsides doing good
And casting demons out.
The Great Physician liveth yet
Thy friend and guide to be;
The healer by Gennesaret
Shall walk the rounds with thee.

This is yet another hymn written by Whitter which is still included in the *Christian Science Hymnal* today. It is on page 229 of the currently used (1932) hymnal.

Mary cured a severe case of pneumonia while the doctor was in the room explaining that the patient was drawing her last breaths. Instead, as Mary herself had done with healing prayers after she fell on the ice, the patient got up, dressed, and joined her family for dinner—her pneumonia gone.

Speaking of this time, Mary Baker Eddy wrote in an essay titled: "To the Christian World":

> *After my discovery of Christian Science, I healed consumption in its last stages. . . . I healed malignant diphtheria and carious bones that could be dented by the finger, saving the limbs when the surgeon's instruments were lying on the table ready for their amputation. I have healed at one visit*

a cancer that had eaten the flesh of the neck and exposed the jugular vein so that it stood out like a chord. I have physically restored sight to the blind, hearing to the deaf, speech to the dumb, and have made the lame walk. . . .

The list of cases healed by me could be made to include hopeless organic diseases of almost every kind. I name those mentioned above simply to show the folly of believing that the immutable laws of omnipotent Mind have not power over and above matter in every mode and form, and the folly of the cognate declaration that Christian Science is limited to imaginary diseases! . . . Without Mind, man and the universe would collapse; the winds would weary, and the world stand still.

The First Church of Christ, Scientist and Miscellany, P. 105.

Certainly the world did not "stand still" for this courageous discoverer. The next forty-four years were very exciting and extremely productive. As for direction, the first verse of one of Mary's poems gives a good indication of what she wanted. This poem is today a hymn and appears in many Christian hymnals, not just the one used by the Christian Science Church.

Shepherd, show me how to go
  O'er the hillside steep,
How to gather, how to sow, —
  How to feed Thy sheep;
I will listen for Thy voice,
  Lest my footsteps stray;

I will follow and rejoice
All the rugged way.

I haven't been able to discover exactly how many times Mary moved between 1866 and 1870, when she and one of her students (really a kind of intern) moved into the second floor of a private school for girls in Lynn and advertised as spiritual healers. But I can safely say she had to move more than twenty times! She didn't have much by then—an old trunk for her clothes, a chair, a portfolio for her papers, and a rolled up straw mat she could put down to protect the floor in whatever room she rented.

Yet, she persisted—writing, teaching, healing—and, by 1875, had a manuscript explaining her discovery ready for printing. As she explained, "This was the first book, recorded in history, which elucidates a pathological Science purely mental."

Rudimental Divine Science, Pp. 16-17.

She stated that while taking her first footsteps in Christian Science Mind-healing, she had to deal with: "timidity, self-distrust, friendlessness, toil, agonies, and victories." This required, she explained, "miraculous vision to sustain her." She also cited meekness, selflessness, and love as necessary footsteps. These, too, were qualities wonderfully expressed by several other courageous women living at the same time as Mrs. Eddy.

Clara Barton (1821-1912) was born on Christmas day the same year as Mary in the farm town of Oxford, Massachusetts. Clara taught school for eighteen years, starting when she was sixteen. But when the Civil War began, she went to the battlefields on her own initiative to bring supplies to wounded soldiers. She became a forceful advocate for a radical change in nursing from doctor-assistant to putting-the-patient first. She provided for disaster relief services throughout the United States by founding the American Red Cross. She wrote four books: three about the Red Cross work, and her autobiography, *Story of My Childhood*.

In 1906, when Clara Barton was interviewed by a magazine writer, she was asked her opinion of Mary Baker Eddy. She replied enthusiastically, "Mrs. Eddy should have the respect and admiration of the whole [United States], for she is its greatest woman. Love permeates all the teachings of this great woman." Mrs. Eddy was equally enthusiastic about Ms. Barton, referring to her in *The Christian Science Journal* as a "soldier, patriot, philanthropist, moralist, and stateswoman."

Susan B. Anthony (1820-1906) studied Christian Science with a pupil of Mrs. Eddy during the time she was internationally famous fighting for women's rights—particularly the right to vote. The Christian Science monthly magazine noted in September 1898, that the eight general officers of the National American Women's Suffrage Association represented six religious denominations. Ms. Anthony, president, was a Quaker, the vice-president a Methodist, and the corresponding secretary a Christian Scientist. The other denominations were Unitarian, Episcopalian, and Congregationalist.

Sarah Hale (1788-1879), another New Hampshire native, edited the first national magazine beginning in 1837, and continued the work for forty more years. It was Sarah Hale who convinced

President Lincoln that the nation should celebrate a special day of Thanksgiving in 1865; and Mary Baker Eddy, after she founded the Christian Science Church, established a special church service for Thanksgiving Day.

Manual of The Mother Church, P. 123.

Sarah Hale helped organize Vassar College, the first school of collegiate rank for girls, and started the first day nursery for children of working mothers. It was she who helped preserve both Bunker Hill in Boston and George Washington's home at Mount Vernon, Virginia.

At this same time, Florence Nightingale (1820-1910) was pioneering ideas about nursing and spirituality. Through her nursing work she grew to believe that there was no conflict between science and spirituality. When she left England in 1854 for the Crimea to organize and supervise hospitals for some 5,000 wounded soldiers, she had a team of only thirty-eight nurses. She is reported to have worked day and night some twenty hours at a stretch, and was acknowledged to have brought order out of chaos. When Mrs. Eddy wrote her textbook, *Science and Health*, she made reference to Florence Nightingale's extraordinary accomplishments.

Sevastopol, Crimea, 1854. The illustration is from *The Sevastopol Sketches*, Tolstoy's account of the war.

Science and Health, P. 385.

Elizabeth Blackwell (1821-1910) was born in England and emigrated to the United States when she was a child. As a young woman in 1847, she was appalled by the high death rate of women in childbirth, and applied to Geneva College, a medical school, to become a doctor. Up to that time no woman had ever been admitted to a medical school in the United States. She graduated two years later at the head of her class. She then went to Europe for further study where she became a colleague of Florence Nightingale.

Lucretia Mott (1793-1880), another New Englander, and Elizabeth Cady Stanton (1815-1902) worked tirelessly for women's rights, and it was they who, in 1848, organized the first women's rights convention at Seneca Falls, New York. Mrs. Stanton, discussing what led up to this convention stated:

"The general discontent I felt with woman's portion as wife, mother, housekeeper, physician, and spiritual guide . . . impressed me with a strong feeling that some active measures should be taken to remedy the wrongs of society in general and of women in particular." It was after Ms. Mott, a leader in the anti-slavery movement in the United States was denied the right—only because she was female—to attend the World Anti-Slavery Convention in 1840 in London, that she turned her wholehearted attention to women's rights, including the right of women to manage their own financial affairs.

The struggle for women's rights was of special importance to Mary Patterson. Even though Dr. Patterson left Mary in 1866, he never sought a divorce from her. And as she began to become wealthy through the sale of her books and her teaching, she realized that it was necessary to divorce him so that when she died he would not inherit her estate. In those days, a woman did not have the right, if she was married, to give her money and goods away to anyone other than her husband. She got her divorce in 1873.

CHAPTER SEVEN

Fame and Fortune

In "Inklings Historic," a short essay she wrote in 1896, Mary Baker Eddy told of what she had accomplished in the thirty years since 1866. I have made a list from what she wrote.

Miscellaneous Writings, P. 382-384.

- She discovered the Science of Christianity.
- She restored the first patient healed in this age by Christian Science.
- She taught the first student in Christian Science Mind-healing.
- She was both the author and publisher of the first books on Christian Science.
- She obtained the first charter for the Christian Science church.
- She originated the church's first form of government.
- She was the first pastor of the Christian Science church.
- She donated to this church the land in Boston on which the first building was built in 1894.
- She obtained the first and only charter for a metaphysical medical college.
- She was the college's first and only president.

✣ She was editor of the first Christian Science magazine.

✣ She inaugurated the church's denominational form of Sunday services and Sunday School.

✣ She ordained, in 1895, that the Bible and *Science and Health with Key to the Scriptures* be the pastor of all churches of the Christian Science denomination.

✣ She insisted that women be equal with men throughout the church organization, and that the readers from the Bible and the textbook be, when possible, a man and a woman.

What a woman! How did she go from having to beg for food and lodging to fame and fortune? Not quickly or easily.

She began healing others immediately after her own remarkable recovery, and she quickly began finding those who wanted her to teach them how they, too, could heal using her spiritual method. She advertised in a Lynn newspaper, saying that if either patients or pupils were not satisfied, they could have their money back.

Often she let men and women study with her in exchange for food or housing, or the promise of payment, when and if they became successful healers using Christian Science.

Retrospection and Introspection, P. 50.

For those who could pay, the tuition was steep. Three weeks of study with Mrs. Glover—twelve lectures—cost more than a term at Harvard. The first time she taught, even before she established the metaphysical college, she had six pupils who paid $100 each. Beginning with the second class, the full charge was $300. That was in 1870; in today's money, that would be more than $3,000.

From 1869 through 1875, the working title of the book that eventually would be named *Science and Health with Key to the Scriptures* was *The Science of Life*. This early version was refused by several Boston publishers and had to be printed privately. There's an interesting story about one of Mary's trips from Lynn to Boston to visit her printer.

She started out from her home one day to get to the train station, where the cost of the ride into Boston was five cents. But she was about half way between her home and the station when a storm came up, and a man driving a team of four horses pulling an empty hearse drew up beside her and offered her a ride.

She climbed up onto the box, which had a cover over it, and discovered that he was headed into Boston to pick up a body not far from where the printer was located and bring it back to Lynn for burial. So he offered to take her all the way into the city right to her printer.

The driver kept a diary, and his son, who later carried on the funeral business, when he learned about the growth of Christian Science, dug into his attic to see what his father's diary might say about his time with Mary Glover. He found the reference, and it said, essentially:

> *Today, I gave a ride into Boston to the most remarkable woman. She was taking a manuscript to a printer, and I politely asked her what it was about. For the next hour she told me of what she had discovered. The time flew by. Mark*

my words, she will be famous one day and that book will be one of the most important ever written.

Manual of The Mother Church, P. 88-93.

Today, the Massachusetts Metaphysical College meets once every three years to prepare up to thirty teachers of Christian Science, but when Mary Glover was the teacher, she held classes every few weeks. Sometimes the lessons took place in the evenings to accommodate those with full-time day jobs. Sometimes the students had to devote several weeks to the study.

And before long, pupils were coming not just from New England but also from throughout the United States and across the Atlantic Ocean.

Of course, all who studied with her were not successful healers. Some wanted to combine medicine with prayers; some were only interested in getting rich; some were confused by what she taught; some were annoyed at the moral life she required of her students, including the giving up of alcohol and tobacco.

As Mary Baker Eddy repeatedly asserted, whoever learned the letter (or written message) in her textbook, in order to demonstrate Christian Science, also had to understand its spiritual significance. Repeating the words she required her pupils to memorize was not enough, and the pupils who quoted mere words or theories would fail to heal. A spiritual awakening, she insisted, was absolutely necessary.

How to get this spiritual view? "Work, work, work, watch and pray," was her answer!

At first, Mary Glover was sure that, as soon as she could describe Christian Science clearly enough in a book, both the religious and medical fields would welcome her discovery and accept her ideas. Medical doctors would use Mind as medicine instead of chemicals and herbs. And homeopathic physicians would use Christian Science instead of "suggestion" or hypnotism to heal patients.

She was sure that the Christian churches, which long had agreed that prayer could heal sin, would now see that it could heal sickness as well, and that sin and sickness often, as Christian Science explained, had the same roots. Therefore, she welcomed into the Massachusetts Metaphysical College pastors and ministers from various Protestant denominations.

In 1876, on Independence Day, Mary Glover and six of her pupils formed the Christian Science Association. When they held a Sunday service, they invited a pastor to address them, many of whom were pastors in their own church organizations. What Mary was discovering was the need for her to found her own church. But she was very reluctant to take this step.

Retrospection and Introspection, Pp. 52- 53.

And so, her first church government called for pastors, and Mary, of course, was the first pastor of her little group of faithful pupils. The numbers of Christian Scientists, particularly when her first, second, and third editions of *Science and Health* were in circulation, grew and grew, and groups of Christian Scientists formed in towns and cities all over the United States.

Some of the men and women chosen to be pastors of this new

denomination had been pastors in Protestant churches; some even were active in Hebrew synagogues. They brought to their Christian Science church services a mixture of what they had believed previously and what they were learning from Mary's writings.

It was a mess.

Christian Scientists were arguing about what was and was not true. They were suing each other and taking Mary to court, and the majority of medical doctors and religious leaders of the day were up in arms arguing against this upstart denomination.

There were those who thought Mary a saint, and those who thought she was a devil. And there were a good many, as the denomination grew in number, who wanted the organization to be a hierarchy so that they could be on the top. That is, they wanted a leader, sub-leaders, lieutenants serving the sub-leaders, and so on.

As Mary's writings about Christian Science Mind-healing began circulating more and more widely, she and her radical ideas came under attack. Ministers, priests, and rabbis warned their congregations not to believe what she had discovered. Newspapers and magazines ridiculed her and made up lies about her personal life. Theologians disagreed with her in speeches as well as in pamphlets.

To be ignorant of one's ignorance is the malady of the ignorant.

Amos Bronson Alcott

In the middle of all this controversy, Mary had a visit from Louisa May Alcott's father, Bronson Alcott, a famous New England philosopher. He praised her originality, acknowledged her metaphysical scientific studies, and encouraged her to forge ahead, regardless of public criticism.

Another writer—and you've probably read at least one of his books—Mark Twain, at first didn't give Mary any support but made fun of her and of her teaching. Later, he apologized. But it was a measure of the fame that came to this once sick, homeless, and poverty-stricken widow that Samuel Clemens (Mark Twain's real name) even bothered to notice what she had written.

When she had earned enough money, and while she was living in the Boston area, she sent money to her son, then in South Dakota, to come and visit her. It was the first time they had seen each other in twenty-three years. Georgy told his mother that his precious daughter had been born with crossed eyes; Mary Glover prayed for her, and when Georgy got back home, he was thrilled to find that her eyes were corrected.

This "distance" healing, sometimes called "absent treatment," was one aspect of Christian Science that many found hard to believe. This was particularly true for those early students of Christian Science who wanted to physically touch their patients, rubbing their heads or touching the spot on the body the patient said was causing pain.

But Mary also traveled miles to talk about Christian Science and to heal patients. One time, when she went to Rhode Island to give a talk, she learned that a friend of her hostess was dying in childbirth, having been harmed internally from surgery the last time she gave birth. The physician had left the patient, telling her family and friends the case was hopeless.

Mary wrote: "I had stood by her side about fifteen minutes

Retrospection and Introspection, P. 40.

when the sick woman rose from her bed, dressed herself, and was well. . . . her babe was safely born, and weighed twelve pounds. The mother afterwards wrote to me, 'I never before suffered so little in childbirth.' "

What happened because of this, unfortunately, was typical. Again, in Mary's own words: "This scientific demonstration so stirred the doctors and the clergy that they had my notices for a second lecture pulled down, and refused me a hearing in their halls and churches. This circumstance is cited simply to show the opposition which Christian Science encountered. . . ."

Retrospection and Introspection, P. 42.

Now, Mary Glover was still a pretty woman. With her health restored, those eyes sparkled, and many of the men who came to study with her found her attractive. Not a few thought she might marry them, and as her fame increased, so did her suitors.

Fortunately, a sturdy, morally-strong, spiritually-minded, former Vermont farm lad—Asa Gilbert Eddy, now a salesman for the brand new Singer Sewing Machine Company—came to Lynn to Mrs. Glover, first for healing, and then to take her Metaphysical College course in how to heal.

They were married on the first of January 1877. And forever after Mary used the name, Mary Baker Eddy. Gilbert, as Mary called him, was an enormous help with the running of the Lynn household. He sorted out those clamoring for Mary's attention who had good motives from those who intended to cheat her and to do her harm. He supported her work on the book she was determined not only would make clear what her discovery was, but also help those reading and studying the book to use the discovery to guide their lives in every aspect.

They traveled to Washington, D.C., together in 1881, and there they took rooms in a boardinghouse, where Mary gave lessons in Christian Science and treated patients with Christian Science healing prayers. Gilbert studied copyright laws, which helped secure Mrs. Eddy's writings from copying without her permission, and many of that city's most influential people bought her book and came to her for consultation.

During the Eddys' time in D.C., someone arranged for Mrs. Eddy to go to the federal prison to visit the man who had recently assassinated the twentieth President of the United States, James A. Garfield. She wrote about the encounter:

> *I visited in his cell the assassin of President Garfield, and found him in the mental state called moral idiocy. He had no sense of his crime; but regarded his act as one of simple justice and himself as the victim. My few words touched him; he sank back in his chair, limp and pale; his flippancy had fled. The jailer thanked me, and said, "Other visitors have brought to him bouquets, but you have brought what will do him good."*

Miscellaneous Writings, P. 112.

Five years after they were married tragedy struck. Gilbert Eddy died. Mrs. Eddy insisted on an autopsy, and the physician who carried it out said that he had died of a congested heart.

Mrs. Eddy said that this life-threatening disease was the result of mental poison. Again, the public and the press ridiculed her for making such a claim. But Mrs. Eddy had discovered that the mental governed the physical, not the other way around.

You can be sure that those who disagreed with her discovery really pounced on the fact that, if she was such a great healer, how come she couldn't heal her own husband. She took his passing hard, very hard. She left Lynn by train to stay for the month of August in a farmhouse in Vermont. Soon after arriving, she wrote a letter to one of her pupils, Clara Choate.

> *I am up among the towering heights of this verdant state, green with the leaves of earth and fresh with the fragrance of good will and human kindness. I never found a kindlier people. I am situated as pleasantly as can be in the absence of the* <u>*one true heart*</u> [her underlining] *that has meant so much to me. O, darling I never shall master this point of missing him all the time I do believe, but I can try, and am trying as I must — to sever all the chords that bind me to person or things material.*

Parsons, *The Early History of Christian Science in Vermont,* Pg. 6-7.

Incredible as it seems, while in deep sorrow over the death of Gilbert, "the one true heart," she agreed to give a talk on Christian Science in a local hall, and reported to Mrs. Choate that: "My lecture made a big stir. A Reverend Methodist called on me the next day and talked pretty much all the [morning], and a [medical doctor] talks of studying [with me]."

Mrs. Eddy came back to the Boston area after this rural time-out. She moved from Lynn into the center of Boston. It was then and there that she established the form of her denominational church, replacing a human pastor, priest, or minister with the two books one of which—the Bible—was the basis of her discovery, and the other which explained that discovery: *Science and Health with Key to the Scriptures*.

This is how a Sunday service was organized by this truly original thinker. Two readers (most often one man and one woman) stand in front of the congregation, one to read from the Bible, and one from the Christian Science textbook. A committee, chosen by Mrs. Eddy, would decide on a set of citations [or quotations] from the two books on one of the twenty-six subjects Mrs. Eddy had chosen. Each of these lesson-sermons was divided into six parts, with alternating Bible and *Science and Health* readings.

Manual of The Mother Church, Pp. 120-121.

The readers were not to serve as pastors and tell the congregation what the citations meant or why they were chosen. Each member of the congregation was left free to listen to the readings and to determine for herself or himself the spiritual messages behind the words. This is still the way every Christian Science church service is conducted today in more than seventy nations around the world.

For many reasons, Boston was fertile soil for Mary Baker Eddy's discoveries about Mind-healing. It was the nation's cultural center for arts and letters. Boston had the first public high school, Boston Latin, established in 1635, and the first college, Harvard,

established a year later in 1636. It had the first public library, which opened its doors in 1653, and the first newspaper serving the Colonies beginning in 1704.

. . . there is the country herself, your country, and . . . you belong to her as you belong to your own mother. Stand by her, boy as you would stand by your mother.

Edward Everett Hale
THE MAN WITHOUT A COUNTRY

Edward Everett Hale (1822-1909) was a distinguished Boston author and clergyman who wrote more than 150 books and pamphlets, including his most famous work, *The Man Without a Country*. From 1856 to 1903, he was the pastor of South Congregational Church in Boston. After he met Mrs. Eddy (most likely in 1882), he was recorded by a pupil of Mrs. Eddy's, Hanover P. Smith, to have stated: "She told me more truth in twenty minutes than I have learned before in twenty years."

It was while she was living in Boston, in 1887, that she invited her son, Georgy, to bring his whole family to live. They stayed for six months, but sorely missed their home in the western United States, so they returned home to Lead, South Dakota. Over the next twenty years, Mrs. Eddy provided the Glovers with the gift of a house, a trust fund, money to educate her grandchildren, and when she passed away, a final generous gift.

As Mrs. Eddy's healing and teaching progressed, and the sales of her textbook grew, she began to have enough money to hire workers, and finally, in 1889, she renovated an old farmhouse in Concord, New Hampshire, up the Merrimack River from Bow where she grew up. She moved into this beautiful home, which was also a farm, in 1892. Here, she was able to create perennial flower gardens, a large vegetable garden, and a small orchard.

She named the house in Concord "Pleasant View," and this it

surely had. It was surrounded by beautiful gardens and trees and was home both to her and to several church officials who worked for her fast-growing church.

Pulpit and Press, Pp. 47-50.

Her farm was also home to pigs, Jersey cows, and two types of horses: a pair of work horses (Nelly and Jerry), and carriage horses; first, a matched pair of bays, Prince and Duke, and later matched blacks Princess and Dolly, and after Dolly died, Major. Mrs. Eddy loved taking carriage rides, most often in a carriage pulled by one horse, but she had several carriages, at least one of which used a pair of horses. The vegetable garden, not far from the rear of the house, furnished most of the vegetables for all those living at Pleasant View. Beside the main house, there was a barn, a stable, a coach house, a cottage, and a windmill.

All who had a lunch or supper at Pleasant View remarked on the frequency with which ice cream was the dessert. It was Mrs. Eddy's favorite, and she particularly loved eating the homemade ice cream with fruits from her own garden: strawberries, raspberries, peaches, blackberries, etc. Pleasant View had its own dairy. A short article in Volume III of the *Christian Science Sentinel* tells that the dairy ". . .is fully supplied with cream separators, churns, and butter workers of the latest improved patterns. . . ."

One field, twenty acres in size, was planted in rye, which was then harvested and taken to a local mill. Another, not quite so large, was used for hay, which was stored in the barn as winter feed for the cows and horses. Mrs. Eddy did not have her own chickens, but purchased eggs from a neighbor. She did, though,

believe in recycling: she raised pigs fed with kitchen scraps. She loved flowers, and allowed a local florist to use her greenhouses to grow flowers for sale, as well as to keep Mrs. Eddy's home filled with fresh flowers both from the greenhouse and from the perennial gardens.

One of the Pleasant View workers was very clever, and rigged up some machinery to use to clip the lawn pulled by one of the work horses. To keep the horse's shoes from digging up the lawn, he fashioned leather boots, which he tied on the four hooves.

Bit by bit, Mrs. Eddy found workers both for church affairs and to take care of the Pleasant View home and farm. In 1898, one of her pupils, named Joseph Mann, offered to oversee the estate. His sister came, too, as a housemaid, and one of his brothers came to be the coachman. From 1901 until Mrs. Eddy left Pleasant View, a young farmer from Kansas, John Salchow, was the number one handyman and farm manager. He was a "Jack of all trades," and one time, when Mrs. Eddy caught a heel on a new carriage step with open ironwork, nothing would do but for John Salchow to heat up the forge he had built and shape a new step.

As her fortune grew, Mrs. Eddy learned how to handle her own accounts, and the land purchases she made and the municipal bonds she invested in all prospered.

A man named Calvin Frye studied at the Massachusetts Metaphysical College with Mrs. Eddy in 1882, and immediately she hired him to be her personal secretary. He kept that post for the next twenty-eight years.

Why did she need a full-time secretary? Why did she hire Calvin Frye? Even before TV and talk radio and e. mail and chat rooms, there were newspapers, magazines, neighbors, and letters. Mrs. Eddy's startling ideas went around the world quickly. When she was invited to preach in a large Boston church, there was standing room only.

She got letters from people who wanted her to heal them, from those who wanted to agree with her, from those who disagreed, and from those who claimed to have discovered Christian Science before she did. She received hundreds of letters weekly. And this kept Calvin Frye very busy. Later, when Christian Science was even better known, Mr. Frye had secretaries to help him, and Mrs. Eddy appointed a spokesman for the church in every state, and in every nation in the world where there was a Christian Science church. They helped her by answering challenges in the press, the courts, and the legislatures.

There is an interesting story about Calvin Frye in 1888, when Mrs. Eddy's home and business office were located in a four-story house in the middle of Boston.

The stairs from the ground floor to the basement kitchen were very steep and Calvin tripped on his way down one morning and because his hands were full, he landed on his neck and broke it. The first person to get to him was sure he had been killed instantly.

Mrs. Eddy flew down three flights of stairs and sat on one of the steps beside him. She spoke aloud to him, saying in substance: "Calvin, get up. I need you. Now get up and carry out your duties."

Once again, those who served in Mrs. Eddy's household could testify to her ability to heal as Jesus had.

Calvin got up and continued down the steps as though nothing had happened.

That house, and the two on either side of it, are on Commonwealth Avenue, a half block north of Massachusetts Avenue. The one Mrs. Eddy lived in has an extra story on top; she had it built so she could have a special, quiet place to work on her book, *Science and Health with Key to the Scriptures*. If you go there, stand on the south side of Commonwealth Avenue and you'll notice that all the other buildings are only three stories high, but number 375 has a fourth story.

Parsons, *The Early History of Christian Science in Vermont,* Pg. 19-21.

In 1897, a Vermont farmer's wife was seriously ill, and the physician they called on said he didn't know what to do for her. The farmer had heard about the Christian Science textbook, so he bought a copy, took it to his wife, and told her to read it hoping it might make her well.

She asked how much he had spent for it, and he confessed that it cost him $3.08. His wife was astonished and gave him the dickens, stating: "A fool and his money are soon parted." Then his wife thought to herself that it would be a waste not to read something that had cost so much. As she said, "I thought I must read it, as he had paid so much for it. If it had been only 50 cents or a $1, I would have left it unread."

Of course, you can guess what happened. Again to quote the wife: ". . . I was healed physically and morally, and am today a well woman, doing my own work and instead of my home being of wretchedness it is one of peace and joy."

Then she concluded,"I want to say that if I could not get another copy, a thousand dollars would not purchase this one."

On January 1, 1899, Mrs. Eddy placed a story in the church magazine, *The Christian Science Journal*, that had the following heading: "THE ONLY CHURCH IN THE UNITED STATES BUILT BY CHILDREN." In the small mill town (lumbering) of Schofield, Wisconsin, Miss Mary E. Graves, who had studied Christian Science at the Massachusetts Metaphysical College in 1877 with Mrs. Eddy, started a Sunday school class in her home in 1896. She helped the children organize the church government. She was the First Reader, but a child was the Second Reader, another the treasurer, and another the clerk.

There were several Harney children: Edith, Florence, Helen, Mary, and Alice. And several Glassow children: Cato (?), Margaret, Arthur, Alfred, Oscar, Ruth, and Frank. Three had the family name of Prahl: Carl, Emil, and Johnny. Three were named Rein: George, Josie, and Arthur. And the nineteenth child was Myrtle Clark.

Every Sunday a collection was taken, and by October 1, 1898, there was a surplus in the bank of $9, "whereupon," as the report states, "the children resolved to appoint a building committee and to build the First Church of Christ, Scientist, of Schofield, Wisconsin." The next day a lot was donated, and one of the adults donated $10 to the building fund and another, $25. The children chose the building plan and the materials, and in sixty days they had a church twenty feet by forty feet, with a seating capacity of 100. The treasurer, just fourteen years old, announced at the dedication service on January 1, 1899, that all the construction bills had been paid, and that "they had $2.27 in the treasury."

While today there is no Christian Science church in Schofield (the population is fewer than 3,000), there is a church less than ten miles north in Wausau. Perhaps some of the members of this Christian Science church are the grandchildren of the original children.

By 1891, Mrs. Eddy had added a section to the *Journal* titled "Home and Children Department." It was filled with stories of children being healed by prayer. One Sunday school teacher sent a report to the *Journal* saying that when she asked her pupils, "What is prayer?," one of the children replied, "I think it's talking with God."

Mrs. Eddy put this definition of God in the magazine for the children: "God is our Father and our Mother; our Minister and our Doctor. He is [our] only real relative on earth and in Heaven."

On April 16, 1891, Mrs. Eddy wrote a letter to the Sabbath School children. It began: "My dear little friends." (The word "friends" was underlined in her original letter, as was "this" further on in the letter). She starts off by asking three questions.

> *"Do you know how much I love you? Do you know that God loves you? Do you know that all the ways of loveliness merit affection? Also they make you smart in planning to do*

good — they make you prompt in doing good, and make your motives unselfish; this is best of all. . ." She ended the letter, "Yours in tenderness, Mary Baker G. Eddy."

Let's jump to 1905. Christian Scientists who agree to pray for others on a full-time basis, that is, to make a profession of healing through Christian Science prayers are called "practitioners." In 1905, the little state of Vermont had 16 such healers, with more than 1,000 throughout the United States. Also there were Christian Science practitioners in Europe and Asia.

England	57
Germany	14
Scotland	12
France	08
Ireland	04
Switzerland	04
China	03
Denmark	01
Holland	01
India	01
Norway	01
Philippines	01

The Concord First Congregational Church, the one Mary's

mother's family had established, held a celebration for its 175th anniversary. Mrs. Eddy was invited to attend. She sent them a gift of $500 (about the same as $5,000 today), and a letter saying she could not attend as, "My little church in Boston, Mass., of thirty-six thousand communicants . . . requires my constant attention."

Volume 23 (1905-1906) of *The Christian Science Journal* told of a great honor given Mrs. Eddy. Quoting from the newspaper *The Boston Herald*, the magazine article stated:

> *Concord's esteemed citizen, Mrs. Mary Baker Eddy, came into possession this week, by special messenger from the publishers, of a rare volume, which has received the highest praise of all who have been fortunate to see it.* The Book of the Presidents and Representative Americans, *for such is the title, is a monumental work of unique character, surpassing in beauty and elaborate workmanship anything of the kind which has hitherto been attempted in America. This magnificent publication...consists of biographical sketches, portraits, and autographs of the Presidents of the United States, . . . It is noteworthy that Mrs. Eddy is the only woman whose biography and portrait appear in the historic volume.*

The certificate that came with Mrs. Eddy's personalized copy of this very special book stated that Mrs. Eddy "has been selected as one of one thousand representative citizens of the United States of America, who stand at the head of their respective vocations." Unfortunately, the section on "representative Americans" was never cleared for publication by the National Biographic Society. But had these citizens been included, Mrs. Eddy would not have been the only woman; three others were selected to appear along with such notable men as the first twenty-six presidents (from George Washington through Theodore Roosevelt), Admiral George Dewey, Thomas Alva Edison, Judge John M. Harlan, and Cornelius Vanderbilt.

In May, 1905, Mrs. Eddy told her college students to, "Watch, pray, demonstrate. Released from materialism, you shall run and not be weary, walk and not faint."

The First Church of Christ, Scientist and Miscellany, P. 254.

She was talking about herself! That's what she had done, and that, she knew, was what every sincere student of Christian Science Mind-healing must do to be successful.

We ended Chapter Five with Mrs. Eddy's special prayer for the little children, and will end this chapter with her big children's prayer.

Father-Mother good, lovingly
Thee I seek, —
Patient, meek,
In the way Thou hast, —
Be it slow or fast,
Up to Thee.

Miscellaneous Writings, P. 400.

CHAPTER EIGHT

"Science and Health"

"Son, would you like to ask me any questions about Christian Science?"

"Can I really?"

"Of course you may. I would love to have your questions and will try my best to answer them."

"I only have one. Who is the 'hence-man' in the textbook?"

"The hence-man? Can you be more specific?"

"In the Scientific Statement of Being, it is the 'hence-man' who is spiritual. Who is he?"

Mrs. Eddy must have laughed, if not aloud, certainly within. One of the most often-quoted passages in *Science and Health with Key to the Scriptures* is what she termed "The Scientific Statement of Being," and requested that it be read to the Sunday School children at the close of the Sunday lessons; also that the First Reader read it from *Science and Health* at the close of the Sunday church service.

It was probably 1906, when the conversation took place between a Christian Science Sunday school pupil and the Discoverer of Christian Science on the lawn at Pleasant View, where the teenager had stayed while his mother had an appointment with Mrs. Eddy.

The final sentence of "The Scientific Statement of Being" in that edition of the textbook then stated: "Spirit is God, and man is His image and likeness; hence man is spiritual and not material."

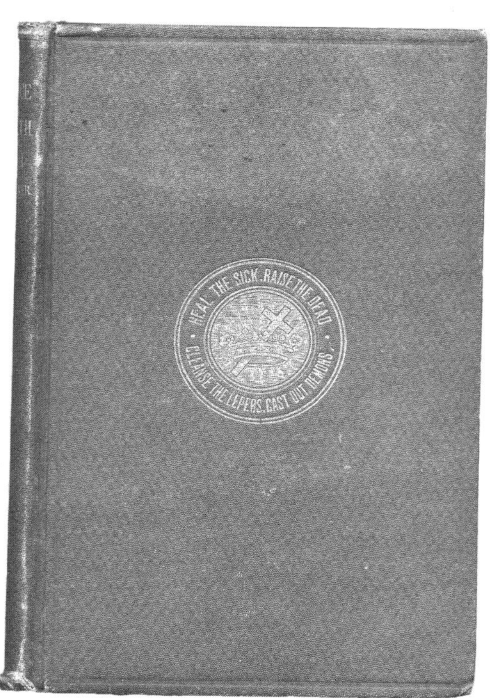

1885 edition of *Science and Health* in which the phrase, "hence man" appears.

Those who already know how this sentence was changed in the last edition of the textbook know that the final sentence now reads: "Therefore man is not material; he is spiritual." (*Science and Health*, P. 468.)

When I was told this story by a teacher of Christian Science, he did so to make two points about Mrs. Eddy. One, that she was humble enough to ask a child for guidance and, two, that she was humble enough to recognize that "therefore" would be a much better choice than "hence." A "henchman," a person who appears in many stories written for children, can be a criminal or a gang member. Certainly Mrs. Eddy did not want anyone, especially children, to be confused and think possibly that the "hence-man," was a "henchman."

To make that one-word change on one page of the textbook, she had to tell the printer to print a whole new book. Now, all the other pages could stay the same, but because *Science and Health* wasn't a looseleaf book, but was bound on the spine, it meant that every change caused another printing.

The first printing of *Science and Health* (1,000 copies) took place in 1875. Mrs. Eddy tried to find a publisher for her book, but each one she showed it to turned it down. So, she raised the money herself and paid for the printing of those first 1,000 copies. Then, when she founded her church, she also founded a publishing house within the church. The first publication of the church, other than the textbook, was a monthly magazine in 1883, which became *The Christian Science Journal*, and many of the articles in it were written anonymously by Mrs. Eddy; that means, she wrote the articles but did not sign her name.

Next came the Bible Lessons in 1890, the ones using the Bible and the textbook for Sunday Christian Science church services. These were printed and mailed all over the world. And eight years later, Mrs. Eddy established a weekly magazine, *The Christian Science Sentinel*.

Meanwhile, she was still working on *Science and Health*. In fact, she spent thirty-one years editing her own book, making changes she was sure would make her explanation about her discovery clearer. She changed the order of the chapters; she made one-word corrections such as from "hence" to "therefore;" she took out portions that had proved to be too controversial or not well enough understood.

Science and Health, Pp. 579-599.

She added a glossary; that is, a chapter explaining her use of key words. For example, "angels." No flying, make-believe creatures for this discoverer. Instead she said that they were, "God's thoughts passing to man; spiritual intuitions, pure and perfect; . . ."

Do students of Christian Science believe in baptism? This is how Mrs. Eddy defines that activity in the glossary: "Purification by Spirit; submergence in Spirit." No water!

"Heaven," she explains, is not a place, but, is "spirituality." And "hell?" Also not a place. She starts that definition with, "Mortal belief; error; lust; remorse; hatred; revenge; sin; sickness; death; suffering and self-destruction; . . ." She may not have made a fire there, but there's nothing good about the "hell" she describes.

From 1881 to 1890, Mrs. Eddy produced fifty different editions of *Science and Health*. Her first two publishers—men who worked directly for her and were paid by her—not only proved to be inept at the work, but also tried to change what Mrs. Eddy ordered. Fortunately, the printer was a skilled and honest man, and he dealt directly with Mrs. Eddy whenever he thought those saying they were speaking for her, actually were speaking for themselves.

By 1906, Mrs. Eddy had made more than 225 revisions; seven were major and occurred between 1878 and 1906. Sometimes she hired professional editors to assist her; other times she called on Christian Scientists to suggest better wording or a different order of the chapters.

In her book *Miscellaneous Writings*, published by the Christian Science Church in 1897, Mrs. Eddy stated: "*Science and Health with Key to the Scriptures* is a complete textbook of Christian Science. . . . There is absolutely no additional secret outside of

Miscellaneous Writings, P. 50.

its teachings, or that gives one the power to heal; but it is essential that the student gain the spiritual understanding of the contents of this book, in order to heal."

Beginning in 1884, Mrs. Eddy placed the following statement in all her books and magazines: "The author takes no patients at present, and has no time for consultation on disease." This discoverer of Christian Science Mind-healing was making yet another discovery: she must found a church to protect *Science and Health*. The formal organization of The First Church of Christ, Scientist, in Boston, Massachusetts, took place September 23, 1892. And on December 30, 1894, the members held their first service in the 1,000-seat church they had spent two years building.

Mary, the sickly farm girl, was now a healthy, world-famous author, a leading religious figure, and the founder of a church dedicated to the use of prayer to meet all challenges from sin, disease, and even the threat of death.

She was prosperous and generous. She also was wise about investments, calling on one of her Baker relatives, a shrewd New England banker, to teach her how to protect her growing estate. She also used the services of lawyers to protect her against slander and fraud. One evidence of her generosity is the gift she gave all children living in and around Concord, New Hampshire, where she was living. Just before the start of each school year, all children who needed a new pair of shoes were invited to come to the local shoe stores, and Calvin Frye, Mrs. Eddy's faithful secretary, followed up by paying for all the shoes.

As her church organization grew and developed, she made significant gifts, such as the excellent location of a plot of land large enough on which to build both the church and the headquarters offices. She also sent a large contribution to Dartmouth College to support Baker Library in memory of her beloved brother Albert.

Mrs. Eddy was the subject of negative articles in newspapers and magazines, as well as a succession of extremely critical books. A New York City dentist, William A. Purrington, wrote a book in 1900 attacking both Mrs. Eddy and Christian Science healing. He asked the reader to judge whether Mrs. Eddy was: "learned, modest, truthful, and generous, or, as her adversaries declare, ignorant, irreverent, boastful, and greedy." Of *Science and Health*, Dr. Purrington alleged that it was filled with "ineffable nonsense." He also referred to it as a "book of jargon" and "dreary."

In a letter to the editor of the *New York Sun* newspaper, on June 9, 1899, Dr. Purrington stated: "Last Sunday afternoon Mr. Carol Norton lectured upon Christian Science at the Metropolitan Opera House. The building was thronged and the audience fairly representative of the average intelligence and education of this city. Although many present were doubtless led thither by curiosity, a very large number, perhaps the majority, were honest believers in the pretensions of Mrs. Eddy."

"Pretensions." This was a common accusation—that Christian Scientists pretended first to be sick and then second to get well through Christian Science Mind-healing. And even though The First Church of Christ, Scientist was a formal legal church, critics constantly referred to it as a "cult," in the same category as voodoo. And often they referred to Christian Science as "Eddyism."

Dr. Purrington made a prediction that the doctrine of Christian Science would disappear. He said: "It does not seem possible that a sane or reverent mind or one with any sense of humor could accept seriously the preachment of the exceedingly shrewd, but very ignorant and ungrammatical old lady, once of Lynn, but now of Concord."

Dr. Purrington was wrong. Not only was Mrs. Eddy taken very seriously, but praise for *Science and Health* was unstinting from the hundreds of thousands who were healed by studying the book and scientifically applying its Mind-healing ideas.

In addition to outside critics such as Dr. Purrington, greed and ambition caused havoc within the developing Christian Science Church. That textbook was a best-seller! Mrs. Eddy wrote another sixteen books that also sold well. The church's magazines were popular, and each month there were more subscribers. Practitioners and churches around the world paid to have their advertisements in the monthly *Christian Science Journal*.

Mrs. Eddy not only had to keep her publishing house productive, but also had to decide what her church organization would be like. She was in charge of it all. Her days (and nights) were filled with:

✣ Teaching Christian Science Mind-healing to pupils who would, after several years of giving full time to healing solely through prayer, become teachers themselves.

✣ Deciding what rules should govern The First Church of Christ, Scientist, and its branches in towns and cities around the world by compiling what she named the *Manual of The First Church of Christ, Scientist*.

✣ Choosing the officers who would serve as publisher, clerk, and treasurer of the church and, until the board of directors was formed, supervising their activities.

✣ Choosing the directors of the church who were to serve as guardians and stewards, overseeing the headquarter's officers, and carrying out the business of the church's central administration, but not to direct the branches.

✣ Choosing the trustees to direct the work of The Christian Science Publishing Society. For more than fifteen years, Mrs. Eddy appointed the editor in charge of the religious magazines and supervised his/her work. She had to dismiss several of the first men who served as editors because they did not state Christian Science correctly. It was a woman, Annie Knott, who was the first editor—beginning in 1903—whose work was acceptable to Mrs. Eddy.

✣ Purchasing the property, then appointing a committee to build and furnish first the original Mother Church building (1893-1894), and then the extension in 1906 to seat some 4,000 to 5,000.

The First Church of Christ, Scientist and Miscellany, Pp. 67-69.

✣ Choosing solid healers and good orators to lecture about Christian Science and tell the truth about Mary Baker Eddy and her discovery primarily in the English-speaking world, but eventually throughout the world.

✣ Choosing well-educated Christian Scientists to serve in

designated regions as official spokesmen for Christian Science, correcting misstatements given by writers or lecturers.

The First Church of Christ, Scientist and Miscellany, P. 353.

✣ Establishing a non-religious, international daily newspaper, *The Christian Science Monitor*, with the motto, "To injure no man, but to bless all mankind."

Speaking with a member of her household thirty years after founding the Christian Science church, Mrs. Eddy explained, "I prayed [to] God day and night to show me how to form my church, and how to go on with it. I understand that He showed me, just as I understand He showed me Christian Science, and no human being ever showed me Christian Science. Then I have no right or desire to change what God has directed me to do, and it remains for the church to obey it."

Dickey, *Memoirs of Mary Baker Eddy,* Pp. 115-116.

Mrs. Eddy faced a very difficult challenge as hundreds found healing of sin, sickness, and even death through studying the Science she discovered. Some of her pupils claimed that she was, as one wrote to her, ". . .greater than Jesus Christ."

She considered this view of her as devastating to the solid growth of Christian Science as the declaration that she was a witch or a devil. Just as she would think her followers understood her place as Discoverer, she would learn of one who was giving speeches claiming divinity for her.

There was a woman teacher of Christian Science in New York City who kept comparing Mrs. Eddy to Jesus. Mrs. Eddy wrote her a severe letter. It says, in part:

> *Awake and arise from this temptation . . . allowing your students to deify . . . me. Treat yourself for it and get your students to help you rise out of it. It will be your destruction if you do not do this. Answer this letter immediately.*

The First Church of Christ, Scientist and Miscellany, P. 359.

In Boston, a man who was a teacher of Christian Science, so convinced his pupils that God had deliberately "chosen" Mrs. Eddy that they believed when she died that she sat on God's left hand, while Jesus sat on His right.

The God Mrs. Eddy discovered doesn't have a lap or sides! Look back at Chapter Six to read her definition of God.

This Boston teacher and his family wrote a will stating that the Christian Science Church could have millions of dollars if—and only if—the church published and authorized a book he wrote about Mrs. Eddy and a Bible prophecy.

Mrs. Eddy anticipated the possibility that incorrect writings about Christian Science would appear and insisted in the set of laws governing the Church (*Manual of the First Church of Christ, Scientist*, P. 43) that a member ". . .shall neither buy, sell, nor circulate Christian Science literature which is not correct. . . ."

Annie Knott, who studied with Mrs. Eddy in 1887 and became a practitioner and then a teacher of Christian Science, was one of those spokesmen chosen by Mrs. Eddy to answer criticism in the press, and to protect the constitutional right of Christian Scientists to religious freedom as healers by working directly with state

legislators. Annie Knott helped draft such protective legislation in Michigan in 1897.

In 1898, Mrs. Eddy appointed Annie Knott as the church's first woman lecturer. A year later, Mrs. Knott met with Mrs. Eddy to explain that she had had few calls to lecture and thought it was because she was a woman. To this Mrs. Eddy replied, "You must rise to the altitude of true womanhood, and then the whole world will want you. . . . Who reflects the most intelligence, the man or the woman? Take Adam and Eve, was it not the woman who first discovered that she was in error and was the first to admit it?"

Annie Knott, writing about this conversation with Mrs. Eddy explained, "To me this was a new definition of intelligence, and I never lost sight of it. The result of her talk was indeed wonderful, for within a short time I began to have numerous calls to lecture . . . and to prove that a woman can declare the truth and heal the sick as well as a man."

We Knew Mary Baker Eddy, Third Series, Pp. 82-83.

Mrs. Eddy loved children, and during the time that devoted Christian Scientists were raising funds to build the original church building, a group of some 2,600 children under the age of twelve, who took the name "Busy Bees," did little chores to raise money specifically to send to Boston to pay for the cost of building a special room in the church's tower—a kind of study room and office for Mrs. Eddy to use. On the dedication day (January 7, 1895) for what was then and still is called The Mother Church, as many Busy Bees as could get to Boston, wearing white patches with a Busy Bee logo in the shape of a bee hive, sat together for the 10:30 a.m. church service. All together they had earned and given to the building fund $4,460!

Later that year, Mrs. Eddy published a small book that included the formal talk she prepared for the dedication service, the hymns that were sung, and copies of the stories about the building of the church that appeared in twenty-four newspapers. She also listed the names of sixty-eight other papers that had carried stories about the building of The First Church of Christ, Scientist in Boston, Massachusetts.

She named the book *Pulpit and Press*, and dedicated it to the Busy Bees.

Dorothy Baldwin had one of these Busy Bee beehive banks made of wood.

Sixty years later, I met and talked with one of those Busy Bees, Mrs. Dorothy Baldwin Garretson, who had come with her mother all the way from England to be in The Mother Church on January 7, 1895. She told me about Mrs. Eddy setting up a trust fund for all the Busy Bee children. Dorothy put all her change in a beehive-shaped bank her mother gave her, and when she was twenty-one she received her share from the trust. Mrs. Garretson also told me about the letter she and all the other children had received from Mrs. Eddy in 1897. I will quote from part of that letter:

See: *The First Church of Christ, Scientist and Miscellany,* Pp. 216-217.

> *Dear Children: As you grow older, advance in the knowledge of self-support, and see the need of self-culture, it is to be expected you will feel more than at present that charity*

> *begins at home, and that you will want money for your own uses. . . . You will want it for academics, for your own school education, or, if need be, to help your parents, brothers, or sisters.*
>
> *Further to encourage your early, generous incentive for action, and to reward your hitherto unselfish toil, I have deeded in trust to The Mother Church of Christ, Scientist, in Boston, the sum of four thousand dollars to be invested in safe municipal bonds for my dear children contributors. . . . This sum is to remain on interest till it is disbursed in equal shares to each contributor. . . . when the contributors shall have arrived at legal age, and each contributor will receive his dividend with interest. . . .*

You are, perhaps, wondering what happened to the $460, since Mrs. Eddy put $4,000 into the trust, and by the time of the dedication service the Busy Bees had given $4,460. Actually, it was even more, as it took some time for all the money coming from around the world to get to the church treasurer. The final total was $5,568.51! Mrs. Eddy suggested that the difference between the $4,000 she put in trust for the children and the $5,568.51 be given to the Christian Science Church then under construction in Concord, New Hampshire. Sunday school children from Christian Science churches throughout the world sent word back to Mrs. Eddy that they would love for the money they earned to go to the Concord church.

It must have given Mrs. Eddy considerable joy to think about innocent children during the early years of the founding of The Church of Christ, Scientist, since she was the subject of so much public ridicule and in-fighting among her headquarter's staff.

Mrs. Eddy loved taking drives in one of her horse-drawn carriages. She had several, some that were open—for good warm weather—and several that were closed, with large windows. All the time she lived at Pleasant View, and for the last two years in the Chestnut Hill section of Boston, she took daily drives, generally with Calvin Frye accompanying the driver. When a newspaper reported that she had died and that the church officials were afraid to tell the world she had, the false accusation was made that a woman in her household was impersonating her on these drives.

The following appeared on March 5, 1905, in the newspaper, *The New York Herald*:

> *Dear Mr. Editor: — A representative of the* Herald *called to-day to inform me of the rumor that I had deceased some three months ago. This is an oft-repeated falsehood. I granted him a moment's interview, hoping you would refute this rumor in the next edition of your paper. I am in my usual good health, drive out every day, and attend to my regular business.*
>
> [Signed] *Mary Baker Eddy*

The reporter described how she looked: "Mrs. Eddy came toward me and extended her hand in greeting. As Mrs. Eddy spoke

her face lighted sweetly, a motherly expression, and the brightness of the large, full eyes bespoke the owner's mental activity. Her tall figure was exquisitely gowned in black silk of becoming and modish cut. Her welcome was cordial. . . ."

A group of former members of the Christian Science church were determined to force Mrs. Eddy out as the leader and to gain control of both her personal wealth and the church's funds. They got newspapers to report that she was too sick to take the carriage rides, and it was they who were the fomenters of the lies about an impostor. They charged that she was too forgetful to be in charge of financial investments. They even got her son to agree to be named as one of those seeking a court order giving them control over her affairs.

As a result of their accusations, a group of lawyers was engaged by the court to go to her home, Pleasant View, and report back to the court whether or not Mary Baker Eddy was incompetent. This challenge took place in 1906, when Mrs. Eddy was eighty five years old. The lawyers were astonished at how physically and mentally well she was, and the suit was dismissed. One of the men said of her after the visit, "She's smarter than a steel trap." The official judicial conclusion was given in more formal terms: "We submit that Mrs. Eddy has a legal right to a finding of her competency."

She held no grudge and soon after gave $245,000 to her son.

She had done what she set out to do. She'd discovered a way to pray that was scientific; she'd founded a church to protect her discovery; and she was now assured that her discovery was safely within the pages of *Science and Health with Key to the Scriptures*.

Mary Baker Eddy passed away quietly in her sleep on December 3, 1910, from what the required medical examiner stated were "normal causes." All of Mrs. Eddy's relatives, and Gilbert Eddy, were buried in Tilton, New Hampshire, but Mrs. Eddy chose the Mount Auburn cemetery in Cambridge, Massachusetts, one designed by Edward Everett (1740-1865).

The Mount Auburn cemetery, dedicated in 1831, was the first of its kind in the United States. Everett was a scholar, a diplomat, and president of Harvard University. His concept was to place the graves within a garden, emphasizing life instead of death. Some 30,000 people visited Mount Auburn annually at the turn of the century marveling at its beauty.

In 1849, President Everett took a Harvard visitor to the cemetery. She wrote in her report, "The finely diversified grounds occupy about 100 acres, in general profusely adorned with a rich variety of trees, and in some places planted with ornamental shrubbery; there are some tombs graced with charming flower-beds. . . ."

In 1863, just one year before his passing and burial in Mount Auburn, Edward Everett along with Abraham Lincoln, gave dedicatory addresses at another garden-like cemetery, patterned after Mount Auburn, in Gettysburg, Pennsylvania. Everett spoke for more than an hour; Lincoln for less than five minutes. But it is Lincoln's speech —known as the "Gettysburg Address"—that is so very famous.

Mrs. Eddy's location is a rotunda "graced with charming

flower-beds." When I took a young teen to visit Mount Auburn and to see Mrs. Eddy's site, she began laughing when she saw which flowers had been planted by the Christian Science Church gardeners. "Impatiens, that's no flower for Mrs. Eddy. She was patience itself, spending all those years explaining her discovery."

Remember, it was Mary Baker, the young scientist, who wanted to learn what it was that made Jesus such a successful healer through prayer alone. She kept on asking herself: "How did he and his followers do those healings?"

She found the answer. It is, of course, in her textbook. The following statement summarizes that discovery about the man known as the "Saviour," or "Wayshower" to Christian Scientists:

> *Jesus beheld in Science the perfect man, who appeared to him where sinning mortal man appears to mortals. In this perfect man the Saviour saw God's own likeness, and this correct view of man healed the sick.*

Science and Health, Pp. 476-477.

APPENDIX

Important Dates

1821 Born on a large farm in Bow, New Hampshire, sixth and last child of Mark and Abigail Baker

1836 Baker family move to a small farm in Sanbornton, NH

1838 After a big disagreement with her father, joins the Congregational Church

1841 Her beloved and brilliant brother Albert dies

1843 Marries George Glover and moves to South Carolina
Husband dies six months later in North Carolina
Moves back to Sanbornton to live with her parents

1844 Son, George Washington Glover II, born

1848 Bakers stop farming and move into town of Sanbornton

1849 Mother dies

1850 Father remarries; Mary moves to her sister Abigail's home
Sister refuses to have six-year-old George in her home
He is boarded out to a family who moves to Franklin, N.H.

1853 Marries Dr. Daniel Patterson, a dentist
Moves to Franklin, N.H. for two years
Son still boards out—visits mother only occasionally

1855 Moves to North Groton, N.H.
Is very ill for the next eleven years
Dr. Patterson is unfaithful to the marriage
They are very poor

1856 Son, now twelve, goes to Minnesota with his adopted family
Son told his mother has died
Mary tries many natural cures
Mary goes on a bread and water diet

1860 Patterson home and goods, which includes all of Mary's furniture and jewelry, taken in bankruptcy
Both move to Rumney, N.H.
Both very poor; husband frequently absent
Mary searches for and cannot find her son

1864 Pattersons move to Lynn, Massachusetts

1866 Discovers the science behind Jesus's healings
Heals herself and begins healing many others
Begins writing about the Science of Christian healing
Begins teaching others to heal through scientific prayer
Husband deserts Mary; this time not to return
The next four years rents rooms in several homes

1870 Moves back to Lynn, Mass. for seven more years

1875 Publishes first edition of her textbook, *Science and Health*

1877 Marries Asa Gilbert Eddy of Londonderry, Vermont
Both of them teach and heal
Continues making editorial improvements on her textbook
Moves to Boston, Mass.

1878 Son, age thirty-four, comes to visit
Mary heals his daughter through prayer of crossed eyes

1880 Publishes third edition of *Science and Health*
Publishes book, *Christian Healing*

1881 Her Metaphysical College chartered
Calvin Frye attends the college, becomes her secretary for the next twenty-eight years

1882 Husband Asa Gilbert Eddy dies
Spends two years looking for a permanent home
Establishes the church founded on her discovery
Names it "The First Church of Christ, Scientist"

1883 Publishes *The Christian Science Journal*, monthly magazine

1887 Publishes *Christian Science: No and Yes*

1888 Publishes *Unity of Good and Unreality of Evil*

1889 Moves to Concord, N.H.

1890 Publishes *Christian Science Quarterly Bible Lessons*

1891 Publishes fiftieth edition of *Science and Health*
Publishes *Retrospection and Introspection*

1892 Final organization of the Church of Christ, Scientist
155 Christian Science churches throughout the world

1895 Publishes the *Manual of The First Church of Christ, Scientist*
Dedicates the building of The Mother Church in Boston
Publishes *Pulpit and Press*

1897 Publishes *Miscellaneous Writings*

1898 Publishes the *Christian Science Sentinel*, a weekly magazine
Founds the Christian Science Board of Lectureship
Has given more than 400 speeches about her discovery

1903 Publishes German edition of *The Herald of Christian Science*, a magazine
Between 1903-1964, *The Herald* is published in (in order):
French, Danish, Norwegian, Swedish, Dutch, Braille, Spanish, Italian, Portuguese, Indonesian, Japanese, Greek

The Herald of Christian Science

"Behold, the tabernacle of God is with men, and he will dwell with them, and they shall be his people, and God himself shall be with them, and be their God."—Revelation 21: 3.

VOLUME I | JANUARY, 1918 | NUMBER 1

Principle and Practice

MARY BAKER EDDY

THE nature and position of mortal mind are the opposites of immortal Mind. The so-called mortal mind is belief and not understanding. Christian Science requires understanding instead of belief; it is based on a fixed eternal and divine Principle, wholly apart from mortal conjecture; and it must be understood, otherwise it cannot be correctly accepted and demonstrated.

The inclination of mortal mind is to receive Christian Science through a belief instead of the understanding, and this inclination prevails like an epidemic on the body; it inflames mortal mind and weakens the intellect, but this so-called mortal mind is wholly ignorant of this fact, and so cherishes its mere faith in Christian Science.

The sick, like drowning men, catch at whatever drifts toward them. The sick are told by a faith-Scientist, "I can heal you, for God is all, and you are well, since God creates neither sin, sickness, nor death." Such statements result in the sick either being healed by their faith in what you tell them—which heals only as a drug would heal, through belief—or in no effect whatever. If the faith-healer succeeds in *securing* (kindling) the belief of the patient in his own recovery, the practitioner will have performed a faith cure which he mistakenly pronounces Christian Science.

In this very manner some students of Christian Science have accepted, through faith, a divine Principle, God, as their savior, but they have not understood this Principle sufficiently well to fulfill the Scriptural command, "Go ye into all the world, and preach the gospel." "Heal the sick." It is the healer's understanding of the operation of the divine Principle, and his application thereof, which heals the sick, just as it is one's understanding of the principle of mathematics which enables him to demonstrate its rules.

Le Héraut de Christian Science

"Voici le tabernacle de Dieu au milieu des hommes! Il habitera avec eux, et ils seront son peuple, et Dieu lui-même sera avec eux."—Apocalypse 21: 3.

TOME I | JANVIER, 1918 | NUMÉRO 1

Principe et Pratique

MARY BAKER EDDY

LA nature et la position de l'entendement mortel sont l'opposé de l'Entendement immortel. Le soi-disant entendement mortel est croyance, non compréhension. La Science Chrétienne demande la compréhension, non la croyance; elle est basée sur un divin Principe, fixe, éternel, absolument indépendant de la conjecture humaine, et il faut qu'elle soit comprise, autrement elle ne saurait être acceptée et démontrée correctement.

La tendance de l'entendement mortel est de recevoir la Science Chrétienne par une croyance au lieu de la recevoir par la compréhension, et cette tendance prévaut comme une épidémie sur le corps; elle enflamme l'entendement mortel et affaiblit l'intellect, mais ce soi-disant entendement mortel ignore absolument ce fait, et chérit par conséquent sa simple foi dans la Science Chrétienne.

Les malades, tels des hommes qui se noient, saisissent au passage tout ce qui flotte vers eux. Le Scientiste de foi dit aux malades: "Je puis vous guérir, car Dieu est tout, et vous êtes bien portants, puisque Dieu ne crée ni le péché, ni la maladie, ni la mort." De tels énoncés aboutissent à l'un de ces deux résultats: ou bien les malades guérissent grâce à leur foi en ce que vous leur dites—foi qui ne guérit que comme guérirait le médicament, par la croyance—ou bien l'effet est nul. Si le guérisseur de foi réussit à *gagner* (animer) la croyance du patient en son propre rétablissement, le praticien aura opéré une guérison par la foi, qu'il appellera à tort la Science Chrétienne.

C'est de cette manière que certains étudiants de la Science Chrétienne ont accepté, par la foi, un divin Principe, Dieu, pour leur sauveur, mais ils n'ont pas suffisamment bien compris ce Principe pour accomplir le commandement Scriptural "Allez par tout le monde et prêchez l'évangile." "Guérissez les malades." C'est la compréhension qu'a le guérisseur de l'opération du Principe divin, et son application de ce Principe, qui guérit les malades, de même que c'est notre compréhension du principe des mathématiques qui nous met à même d'en démontrer les règles.

Each edition of the *Herald* was bilingual. English appeared on the left-hand pages and the foreign language on the right facing page.

This is a picture of the first volume of the *French Herald*. It was published in January of 1918.

1906 Publishes final edition of her textbook explaining her discovery

1908 Starts newspaper, *The Christian Science Monitor*
More than 1,000,000 copies of textbook sold since 1875
Moves to Chestnut Hill, a Boston suburb

1910 Mary Baker Eddy dies at home on December 3
More than 1,000 Christian Science churches throughout the world

1912 Between 1912 and 1987, *Science and Health* translated into German, French, Braille, Spanish, Swedish, Dutch, Danish, Italian, Portuguese, Russian, Norwegian, Polish, Greek, Indonesian, Japanese, Czech, Finnish

2000 More than 8,000,000 copies of *Science and Health* sold since 1875

Thank You

Eliana Grinstein-Camacho (Weston, Massachusetts); Cari Chastain (Tampa,Florida); Jasmine and Tristan Linck (Wyoming, Ohio); and Sara Watkins (London, England) are all middle-grade students who are Christian Science Sunday School pupils. I asked them what they would want a biography of Mary Baker Eddy to say about her, and they gave me the most wonderful thoughtful answers. I've tried most sincerely to meet their high goals for this biography.

* Be detailed; tell specific events.
* Explain why, don't just give general comments.
* Didn't she ever wear slacks?
* Why does her hair looks so strange?
* Why and how did she discover Christian Science?
* What was she like as a teenager?

* Tell enough about her so I know whether I would have been her friend.
* Explain what led up to her discovery.
* Did she ever do anything wrong?

After I had written the first draft of the biography, I asked two middle-grade girls who do not go to the Christian Science Sunday School, and who had never read anything about Mary Baker Eddy, to read the draft and tell me whether they found it easy to read, or if the vocabulary was too difficult. I asked them, too, if I had told them enough about her, and whether they understood why she was so famous. I explained that since I was asking them to read the manuscript as professionals, that I would pay them for their editorial review.

Hallie Clark (Mobile, Alabama) was most enthusiastic; said that the vocabulary was "O.K.," and that she thought adults as well as children would enjoy the book. Norma Heller (Lincoln, Nebraska) was very encouraging, also had no trouble with the vocabulary, but felt that she wanted to know a lot more about Mrs. Eddy.

I also asked two professional editors to review the initial draft, and a subsequent draft. Lee Griffin (Winooski, Vermont) is one of those rare editors who sees the big picture while simultaneously correcting the lost parts of speech and wayward phrases. I have worked closely with Lee as an editor since 1982, and continue to grow in admiration of her expertise. Trudi Treworgy Riesenberg,

Ph.D. (Harpswell, Maine), is a life-long Christian Scientist, a sound English scholar, possessor of a keen editorial eye, and a close enough friend for some 55 years that she can point out what needs correcting so firmly and clearly that I am eager to obey.

I thank them one and all for their editorial input. They are only responsible for encouraging me; they are not responsible for any lapses in statement or editorial judgment—these are mine alone.

Alice DeCaprio (Sarasota, Florida), is a life-long Christian Scientist and an accomplished artist. Her sketches, like Alice, are fresh and inspirational. What joy she has brought to this biography! I am sure I am not the only one who says, "Thanks Alice."

The majority of photographs are the generous gift of the Longyear Museum in Chestnut Hill, Massachusetts, to whom I am deeply grateful.

I am grateful, too, for the help I received from a professional book designer. Young readers may not know it, but author and designer often collaborate on what typeface to use, where to place the page numbers, what should be on the cover, and so forth.

I would be remiss if I did not acknowledge, and thank, all those who have written biographies and biographical sketches of Mrs. Eddy; I am particularly grateful for Robert Peel's 3-volume set: *Mary Baker Eddy: The Years of Discovery*, *Mary Baker Eddy: The Years of Trial*, and *Mary Baker Eddy: The Years of Authority*.

And now, a special "thank you" for you readers, for allowing me what is sometimes called an "author's license." Of course, I don't know exactly what Mary Baker's grandmother said to little Mary on page one, and so, in order to use dialog, I have constructed a few conversations based on my reading of more than ten biographies of Mary Baker Eddy. I feel confident that what I have used as dialog is close, very close, to what actually might have been said.

PHOTO BY TERESA HELLER

The author, wearing the black and white blouse, and the first editor, Norma Heller, meet for the first time. Cynthia tells Norma she has memorized her praise for the book: "I absolutely, positively, adore it."

"But Cynthia, I also told you it was too short."

"Yes, I know you did, and I've now added another 10,000 words."

"Good."

THE VERMONT SCHOOLHOUSE PRESS
Chester, Vermont